World Music Pedagogy, Volume I

World Music Pedagogy, Volume I: Early Childhood Education is a resource for music educators to explore the intersection of early childhood music pedagogy and music in cultural contexts across the world. Focusing on the musical lives of children in preschool, kindergarten, and grade 1 (ages birth to 7 years), this volume provides an overview of age-appropriate world music teaching and learning encounters that include informal versus formal teaching approaches and a selection of musical learning aids and materials. It implements multimodal approaches encompassing singing, listening, movement, storytelling, and instrumental performance.

As young children are enculturated into their first family and neighborhood environments, they can also grow into ever-widening concentric circles of cultural communities through child-centered encounters in music and the related arts, which can serve as a vehicle for children to know themselves and others more deeply. Centered around playful engagement and principles of informal instruction, the chapters reveal techniques and strategies for developing a child's musical and cultural knowledge and skills, with attention to music's place in the development of young children. This volume explores children's perspectives and capacities through meaningful (and fun!) engagement with music.

Listening Episode music examples can be accessed on the eResource site from the Routledge catalog page.

Sarah H. Watts is Assistant Professor in Music Education in the School of Music at The Pennsylvania State University.

Routledge World Music Pedagogy Series
Series Editor: Patricia Shehan Campbell, University of Washington

The **Routledge World Music Pedagogy Series** encompasses principal cross-disciplinary issues in music, education, and culture in six volumes, detailing theoretical and practical aspects of World Music Pedagogy in ways that contribute to the diversification of repertoire and instructional approaches. With the growth of cultural diversity in schools and communities and the rise of an enveloping global network, there is both confusion and a clamoring by teachers for music that speaks to the multiple heritages of their students, as well as to the spectrum of expressive practices in the world that constitute the human need to sing, play, dance, and engage in the rhythms and inflections of poetry, drama, and ritual.

Volume I: Early Childhood Education
Sarah H. Watts

Volume II: Elementary Music Education
J. Christopher Roberts and Amy C. Beegle

Volume III: Secondary School Innovations
Karen Howard and Jamey Kelley

Volume IV: Instrumental Music Education
Mark Montemayor, William J. Coppola, and Christopher Mena

Volume V: Choral Music Education
Sarah J. Bartolome

Volume VI: School-Community Intersections
Patricia Shehan Campbell and Chee-Hoo Lum

World Music Pedagogy

Early Childhood Education

Volume I

Sarah H. Watts
The Pennsylvania State University

NEW YORK AND LONDON

First published 2018
by Routledge
711 Third Avenue, New York, NY 10017

and by Routledge
2 Park Square, Milton Park, Abingdon, Oxon, OX14 4RN

Routledge is an imprint of the Taylor & Francis Group, an informa business

Library of Congress Cataloging-in-Publication Data
The Library of Congress has cataloged the combined volume edition as follows:
Names: Roberts, J. Christopher, author. | Beegle, Amy C., author.
Title: World music pedagogy.
Description: New York ; London : Routledge, 2018– | Includes bibliographical references and index.
Identifiers: LCCN 2017050640 (print) | LCCN 2017054487 (ebook) | ISBN 9781315167589 () | ISBN 9781138052727 | ISBN 9781138052727q(v.2 : hardback) | ISBN 9781138052796q(v.2 : pbk.)
Subjects: LCSH: Music—Instruction and study.
Classification: LCC MT1 (ebook) | LCC MT1. W92 2018 (print) | DDC 780.71—dc23
LC record available at https://lccn.loc.gov/2017050640

ISBN: 978-1-138-03893-6 (hbk)
ISBN: 978-1-138-03894-3 (pbk)
ISBN: 978-1-315-17703-8 (ebk)

Typeset in Times New Roman
by Apex CoVantage, LLC

Visit the eResource: www.routledge.com/9781138038943

Contents

Series Foreword

Turning and turning in the widening gyre
The falcon cannot hear the falconer;
Things fall apart; the centre cannot hold;
Mere anarchy is loosed upon the world . . .
(from "The Second Coming," W. B. Yeats)

There is a foreboding tone to the stanza epigraph, which at first may seem out of sync with a book on the pedagogy of world music. After all, music education is an intact phenomenon, arguably innocent and pure, that envelops teachers and their students in the acts of singing, playing, and dancing, and this field is decidedly not about falcons. Instead, music education conjures up long-standing images of spirited high school bands, choirs, orchestras; of young adolescents at work in guitar and keyboard classes; of fourth grade xylophone and recorder players; of first grade rhythm bands; and of toddlers accompanied by parents playing small drums and shakers. At a time of demographic diversity, with a wide spectrum of students of various shapes, sizes, and hues laid wide open, music education can press further, as the field has the potential to hold court in a child's holistic development as a core avenue for the discovery of human cultural heritage and the celebration of multiple identities based upon race, ethnicity, gender, religion, and socioeconomic circumstance.

Yet there is a correspondence of the stanza, and the disquiet that Yeats communicates, with this book and with the book series, *World Music Pedagogy*. I refer the reader to the start of the third line, and also to the title of a novel by Nigerian author Chinua Achebe. A landmark in the world's great literature, *Things Fall Apart* has been very much in mind through the conception of this project, its design and development by a team of authors, and its thematic weave in these tempestuous times. Achebe's writing of cultural misunderstanding, of the arrogance and insensitivity of Western colonizers in village Africa, of competing cultural systems, is relevant.

We raise questions relative to music teaching and learning: Do things fall apart, or prove ineffective, when they do not reflect demographic change, do not respond to cultural variation, and do not reasonably reform to meet the needs of a new era? Can music education remain relevant and useful through the full-scale continuation of conventional practices, or is there something prophetic in the statement that things fall apart, particularly in music education, if there are insufficient efforts to revise and adapt to societal evolution? There is hard-core documentation of sparkling success stories in generations of efforts to musically educate children. Yet there is also evidence of frayed, flailing, and failing programs that are the result of restrictive music selections and exclusive pedagogical decisions that leave out students, remain unlinked to local communities, and ignore a panorama of global expressions. There is the sinking feeling that music education programs exclusively rooted in Western art styles are insensitive and unethical for 21st century schools and students and that choices of featured music are statements on people we choose to include and exclude from our world.

Consider many school programs for their long-standing means of musically educating students within a Western framework, featuring Western school-based music, following Western literate traditions of notation, Western teacher-directed modes of learning, and Western fixed rather than flexible and spontaneously inventive musicking potentials. All good for particular times and places, and yet arguably unethical in the exclusion of music and music-makers in the world. Certainly, all practices deserve regular review, upgrades, even overhauls. Today's broad population mix of students from everywhere in the world press on diversifying the curriculum, and the discoveries of "new" music-culture potentials are noteworthy and necessary in making for a more inclusive music education.

So, the Nigerian author selected the Irish poet's phrase as meaningful to his seminal work, much as we might reflect upon its meaning so to muster a response to the societal disruption and contestation across the land, and in the world. The practice of musically educating children, youth, and adults may not at first appear to be the full solution to the challenges of local schools and societies, nor essential to meeting mandates in cultural and multicultural understanding. But music is as powerful as it is pan-human, musicking is musical involvement in what is humanly necessary, and the musical education of children and youth benefits their thoughts, feelings, and behaviors. When things fall apart, or seem to be on the brink of breaking up, of serving fewer students and to a lesser degree than they might be served, we look to ways in which the music of many cultures and communities can serve to grow the musicianship of our students as well as their understanding of heritage and humanity, of people and places. Thus, from cynicism springs hope, and from darkness comes light, as this book and book series rises up as a reasoned response to making music relevant and multiply useful in the lives of learners in schools and communities.

THE SERIES

Each of the six volumes in the **World Music Pedagogy Series** provides a sweep of teaching/learning encounters that lead to the development of skills, understandings, and values that are inherent within a diversity of the world's musical cultures. Written for professionally active teachers as well as students in undergraduate and certification programs on their way to becoming teachers, these volumes encompass the application of the World Music Pedagogy (WMP) process from infancy and toddlerhood through late adolescence and into the community.

The books are unified by conceptualizations and format, and of course by the Series aim of providing theoretical frameworks for and practical pedagogical experiences in teaching the world's musical cultures. Individual WMP volumes are organized by music education context (or class type) and age/grade level.

For every volume in the World Music Pedagogy Series, there are common elements that are intended to communicate with coherence the means by which learners can become more broadly musical and culturally sensitive to people close by and across the world. All volumes include seven chapters that proceed from an introduction of the particular music education context (and type), to the play-out of the five dimensions, to the reflective closing of how World Music Pedagogy contributes to meeting various musical and cultural goals, including those of social justice through music as well as issues of diversity, equity, and inclusion.

There are scatterings of music notations across each volume, mostly meant to assist the teacher who is preparing the orally based lessons rather than to suggest their use with students. Many of the chapters launch from vignettes, real-life scenarios of teachers and students at work in the WMP process, while chapters frequently close on interviews with practicing music educators and teaching musicians who are devoting their efforts to effecting meaningful experiences for students in the world's musical cultures. Authors of several of the volumes provide commentaries on published works for school music ensembles, noting what is available of notated scores of selected world music works, whether transcribed or arranged, and how they can be useful alongside the adventures in learning by listening.

LISTENING EPISODES FOR THE SERIES

Of central significance are the listening episodes for recordings that are featured in teaching-learning episodes. These episodes are lesson-like sequences that run from 3 minutes to 30 minutes, depending upon the interest and inclination of the teacher, paying tribute to occasions for brief or extended listening experiences that may be repeated over a number of class sessions. The listening episodes are noted in the episode descriptions as well as at each chapter's end, and users can connect directly to the recordings (audio as well as video recordings) through the Routledge eResource site for each of the Series' volumes, linked to the catalog page of each volume through www.routledge.com/Routledge-World-Music-Pedagogy-Series/book-series/WMP.

All volumes recommend approximately 20 listening episodes, and Chapters 2–6 in each volume provide illustrations of the ways in which these listening selections can develop into experiences in the five WMP dimensions. From the larger set of recommended listening tracks, three selections continue to appear across the chapters as keystone selections which are intended to show the complete pathways of how these three recordings can be featured through the five dimensions. These Learning Pathways are noted in full in Appendix 1 so that the user can see in one fell swoop the flow of teaching-learning from Attentive Listening to Engaged Listening, Enactive Listening, Creating World Music, and Integrating World Music. Appendix 2 provides recommended resources for further reading, listening, viewing, and development of the ways of World Music Pedagogy.

***

As a collective of authors, and joined by many of our colleagues in the professional work of music teachers and teaching musicians, we reject the hateful ideologies that blatantly surface in society. We are vigilant of the destructive choices that can be made in the business of schooling young people and that may result from racism, bigotry, and prejudice. Hate has no place in society or its schools, and we assert that music is a route to peace, love, and understanding. We reject social exclusion, anti-Semitism, white supremacy, and homophobia (and other insensitive, unfeeling, or unbalanced perspectives). We oppose the ignorance or intentional avoidance of the potentials for diversity, equity, and inclusion in curricular practice. We support civility and "the culture of kindness" and hold a deep and abiding respect of people across the broad spectrum of our society. We are seeking to develop curricular threads that allow school music to be a place where all are welcome, celebrated, and safe, where every student is heard, and where cultural sensitivity can lead to love.

Acknowledgements

This collective of authors is grateful to those who have paved the way to teaching music with diversity, equity, and inclusion in mind. I am personally indebted to the work of my graduate school mentors, William M. Anderson, Terry Lee Kuhn, and Terry M. Miller, and to Halim El-Dabh and Virginia H. Mead, all of whom committed themselves to the study of music as a worldwide phenomenon and paved the way for me and many others to perform, study, and teach music with multicultural, intercultural, and global aims very much in mind. I am eternally grateful to Barbara Reeder Lundquist for her *joie de vivre* in the act of teaching music and in life itself. This work bears the mark of treasured University of Washington colleagues, then and now, who have helped lessen the distance between the fields of ethnomusicology and music education, especially Steven J. Morrison, Shannon Dudley, and Christina Sunardi. Many thanks to the fine authors of the books in this Series: Sarah J. Bartolome, Amy Beegle, William J. Coppola, Karen Howard, Jamey Kelley, Chee Hoo Lum, Chris Mena, Mark Montemayor, J. Christopher Roberts, and Sarah H. Watts. They are "the collective" who shaped the course of the Series and who toiled to fit the principles of World Music Pedagogy into their various specialized realms of music education. We are grateful to Constance Ditzel, music editor at Routledge, who caught the idea of the Series and enthusiastically encouraged us to write these volumes, and to her colleague, Peter Sheehy, who carried it through to its conclusion.

As in any of these exciting though arduous writing projects, I reserve my unending gratitude for my husband, Charlie, who leaves me "speechless in Seattle" in his support of my efforts. Once again, he gave me the time it takes to imagine a project, to write, read, edit, and write some more. It could not have been done without the time and space that he spared me, busying himself with theories behind "the adsorption of deuterated molecular benzene" while I helped shape, with the author-team, these ideas on World Music Pedagogy.

Patricia Shehan Campbell
December 2017

Acknowledgements

My sincerest thanks are due to the many individuals who assisted with this endeavor. First and foremost, I extend my gratitude to Patricia Shehan Campbell for her guidance and mentorship in this and all of my professional undertakings. My further thanks go to those who assisted in the preparation of this book in myriad ways: my husband, Jonathan Watts; my research assistant, James Eldreth; musical consultant Le Zhang; and my readers, Trish Cerminara, Debora Dougherty, Janice Fanjoy, Trudy Watts, and Marissa Works. I am extremely appreciative of the parents who have allowed their children to be featured in this volume: Ann Clements and Chaz Wall, Keith and Janice Fanjoy, Steven and Daisha Hankle, and Rob and Wendy Watts. I offer my thanks to my mother, Vicki Seel, for her steadfast love and unwavering commitment to support me in all I do. Last, much love to my favorite felines, Frodo, Dobby, and T. Panther.

Episodes

Listening Episode music examples can be accessed on the eResource site from the Routledge catalog page.

1

Teaching and Learning in Context

The preschool music campers are musically hard at work, playing, singing, dancing, listening, and learning about the musical world around them. Their teacher, Mr. Jonathan, beckons them over to the felt board and displays bright color photos of three Japanese instruments: the taiko *drum, the stringed* koto, *and a traditional Japanese flute, the* shakuhachi. *Musical instruments always seem to inspire curiosity in 4- and 5-year-olds—kids are enraptured by new sounds and shapes and compelled by just how these instruments work. The three traditional instruments on the felt board in today's class are no different.*

Mr. Jonathan plays excerpts of music by each of the instruments, asking the children to try to figure out which sound goes with which picture. They accomplish this with ease, tapping into their seemingly innate knowledge of the physics of drums, strings, and flutes, principles of sound they have gleaned throughout their short lifespans and applied to these new sounds. Except the sounds are not new to everyone! Sitting off to the side, seemingly uninterested up until this point, Theo gleefully exclaims "taiko!" *alluding to his familiarity with this particular instrument due to his own Japanese heritage and family engagement with this music. Young children are keenly attuned to the world around them, the many and varied sounds of their cultural environments. They are awash in the tones and timbres of the world and rejoice in the familiar and seek to explore the unfamiliar.*

Music is an essential element of human existence that permeates the lives of young children. All music, from every corner of the world, has the potential to intrigue, excite, educate, and invite little ones to listen and respond in myriad ways. The first chapter of children's lives, especially the period of their infancy, toddlerhood, and preschool years, is an opportune time for developing their joy and wonder of the world and offering them experiences that open their eyes, ears, and minds to the beautiful diversity of cultural, artistic, and musical practices they can know. The soothing sound of a caregiver's lullaby, the tunes and tones of favorite cartoon programs, the creative rhythmic and melodic utterances that accompany imaginary play, all of these contribute to the musical threads woven throughout a young child's life. At this time of peak receptiveness to music, it behooves those who care for and teach young children to consider these early years as an excellent window for bringing the world's musical cultures into children's lives, capitalizing on their existing interest to broaden their aural, social, and cultural awareness. In their early years, young children can grow with eyes and ears wide open into a discovery of the world of music, in music, and through music.

Music is a human art form, an inexorable part of the human experience everywhere in the world. Music is social, and indelibly woven into the tapestry of life, and young children are very much a part of this multifaceted fabric. The musical experiences they have provide opportunities for them know language, behaviors, customs, traditions, beliefs, values, stories, and other cultural nuances. As they become musically skilled through experiences in song and instrumental music, young children can also grow cultural knowledge and sensitivity. Music is a vital aspect of culture, shaping and transmitting the aforementioned aspects that characterize groups of people. Exposing young children to the world's musical cultures brings them into the cultural conversation, allowing them to learn about self and others in an artistically meaningful and engaging way. Prior to the development of social biases and cultural preferences that all too easily devolve into prejudices, the opportunity to know people through song, dance, and instrument play is a gift to all who work for the well-balanced development of young children into the responsible citizens they will one day become.

The Necessity of World Music Pedagogy in Early Childhood

Young children are natural observers—watchers and listeners—who are constantly absorbing the sights and sounds that swirl around them. They observe language, behaviors, faces, vocal inflections, and gestures that help them shape their own identities and viewpoints. At this stage in their development, they are uniquely suited to diving into the world's musical cultures, receiving new sounds and ideas, and engaging in curious pursuit of instruments and musicians who play, sing, and dance. As young children learn through observation and immersion, they are primed for the holistic way in which many of the world's musicians transmit their own traditions and cultural values. Music serves as an enticing entry point for them to know people "near and far" from their own families, and a full sampling of sounds invites their curiosity and involvement in knowing people through the music they make. Observations of young children at play show them in the midst of a multifaceted entity of sounds and movement, of imagination and creativity, a close approximation of the various ways in which culture-sharing groups across the globe manifest their musicking. The musical experiences that young children can have set the stage for their cultural understandings, the development of their musical sensitivities, and their pathways to becoming citizens (and musical citizens) of the world.

Regardless of where they live, young children's lives are wrapped up with musically expressive practices. They are enculturated into music of their cultural surrounds, and they develop musical sensitivities as a result of the music to which they are exposed by parents and extended family members, by their community, and by teachers who offer them journeys beyond their first experiences and into the greater musical world. Research by those in music, education, and the social sciences indicates that young children's interests are expansive and that the rate of their absorption of knowledge is impressive from an early age. Their acceptance of new knowledge knows no bounds, as they are open and receptive to experiences that please them. Thus can young children enjoy and learn from the many musical experiences that enter into their lives.

Despite this common thread of music shared amongst all humans, interpersonal and intercultural biases still manage to emerge. Young children in the early years of their lives are by no means too young to observe and absorb the various prejudices that may be modeled for them in word and deed by their families and caregivers. This reality sheds light on the imperative nature of bringing up young children in a multicultural musical landscape, modeling the possibilities for developing respect and understanding amongst all (musical) beings. World Music Pedagogy aims to head off the development of these biases and prejudices at an early age by giving children equitable exposure to music from around the globe (Campbell, 2004). While young children are developing their musical skills of singing, dancing, and playing, they must also be invited to cultivate the skills of thinking, sharing, empathizing, and developing a wide palette of musical possibilities and creative expressions. Music can be the lynch pin around which these interpersonal skills can unfold. Beyond dealings with pitches, rhythms, and timbres lies the knowledge that all people are rooted in valid and beautiful musical cultures, opening minds to the world's people through music. Young children need the opportunity to learn that all people are unified in their human artistic and aesthetic engagement and that all people are worthy of respect and understanding for what they bring to the table.

An incorrect assumption would be that World Music Pedagogy seeks to exclude the Western European Art Music traditions that are so pervasive across cultures. The intent of World Music Pedagogy is to bring all cultures into the musical consciousness of children, with all traditions considered valid and essential for study and performance. The all-inclusive nature of this pedagogy is, all at once, freeing and overwhelming—with the entire world available for study, where does one begin? It might make the most sense for teachers to begin where they are most comfortable and branch out from there, examining personal and family musical traditions and cultural backgrounds. Friends and colleagues might present new voices and viewpoints of music from their own cultural traditions. The children themselves can even inspire teachers to more deeply explore the musical cultures of the little ones whom they serve. Live performances of the world's musical cultures by teachers and culture-bearers are ideal, but teachers need not worry if these are not possible—effective use of recorded music as presented in this volume, accompanied by singing, dancing, and playing, can draw children into new worlds of sound and appreciation of those who create these sounds.

Early Childhood Music: Its Forms and Functions

One of the most compelling, creativity-inducing aspects of early childhood musical engagement is that it can take on many different manifestations. From the mother singing a lullaby to soothe her baby to sleep, to a toddler music class accompanied by parents or caregivers, to the natural rhythms and tunes that emerge during playtime, young children are doing music in many ways. Teachers might engage young children with music during circle time in the childcare setting (as pictured in Figure 1.1) or use music as a tool for smooth transitions in the Kindergarten classroom, or young children may even attend a music class designed especially for them by a trained music teacher. Early childhood music is often free to operate outside the confines of the traditional public school context, moving into a realm of customization of musical encounters and acknowledgement of the children's contributions.

Young children learn informally—language, behaviors, facial expressions, movement; it makes sense, then, that their music learning encounters are delivered informally as well. In the case of a dedicated music time, the teacher may apply this principle of informal instruction through the facilitation of a musical environment, modeling musical behaviors for children, but not necessarily expecting full participation in return. Children of this age and stage may need or want time to observe and absorb—many times a child will quietly observe a music session only to return home and re-teach the entire lesson to her parents or caregivers!

Teachers of early childhood music must plan and prepare effectively, stepping in front of children with a wealth of engaging activities to capture their attention and imaginations. However, an early childhood music class is also a place to expect the unexpected, where flexibility and improvisation are key skills for the teacher to exercise, depending upon the needs and expressions of the children. A typical class may begin with a greeting or welcome song or activity and may proceed with exploration of the voice, songs, games, movement, engagement with child-friendly instruments, and props such as parachutes, ribbons, or balls, puppets, and other manipulatives. Young children are not pressured to respond or perform, but, rather, are given the model of a way to participate. They may invent their own ways to vocalize or play or move, and the adept teacher will capitalize on those moments, reinforcing and extending the child's musical autonomy.

Early childhood music classes might occur on an ad hoc basis so that students of music and education can grow an awareness of the specialized ways in which music can brighten and enlighten the lives of young children. University-level coursework for pre-service teachers might feature practicum experiences in the early childhood setting, an environment where novice teachers can easily acquire some experience with planning and implementing music instruction (with a very forgiving clientele). In-service teachers, too, who are suddenly charged with teaching music to younger children than had been the focus of their university training, may be drawn to studies in early childhood music education. This may occur through further coursework, professional development conferences, early childhood print resources (like this volume), or even jumping in and trying it out!

Several early childhood music organizations exist and serve children and their families in various capacities. Gymboree offers musical play classes for children ages 6 months through 5 years, tailored to developmental stages. These classes incorporate singing, movement, dance, and instruments while cultivating children's social and physical development. Props like parachutes, scarves, and other child-friendly gym equipment round out the experience. Kindermusik is a popular organization offering music instruction to children and families. Based in research, Kindermusik employs the methodological work of Orff, Kodály, and Suzuki in its sequential lessons. This approach focuses on the whole child, that is, the varying learning domains that a child must cultivate, including language, math, social-emotional intelligence, and creativity. This approach also exposes children to many different musical styles and cultures. Music Together focuses on the development of musical aptitude that all children possess. Largely based in the work of Edwin Gordon and Music Learning Theory, Music Together specializes in music instruction for infants through preschool-age children and beyond. Classes for school-age children are available, as are multi-generational classes to engage the family and community. Musikgarten, additionally, provides early childhood music instruction for young children and their families. With an emphasis on developing the whole child in a holistic manner, Musikgarten focuses on high-quality materials and repertoire, age-appropriate and sequential curriculum, and empowerment of families to bring the content into the home. Many other local or smaller-scale companies are bringing music into children's lives in similar ways, such as the Seattle-based Musically Minded, Inc. (see Teacher Feature in Chapter 5).

More broadly, music most certainly plays a starring role in the day-to-day operation of an early childhood classroom or childcare setting. Songs are sung to encourage swift clean-up of toys, rhythmic chants accompany storytelling and circle time activities, and recorded music soothes young children to sleep during their post-lunch resting time. Several well-known approaches to facilitating early childhood learning are committed to the inclusion of music as a vehicle to cultivate creativity and self-expression. The approach to early childhood education developed by Maria Montessori in Italy around the turn of the 20th century is one intended to empower children to take responsibility for learning and exploration in developmentally appropriate ways. Children engage with compelling and interesting hands-on materials, fostering curiosity and critical thinking (Burns, 2017). Music and culture studies are overtly built into these learning encounters. Children may investigate the wide world through boxes of

Figure 1.1 A music class for toddlers

manipulative and artifacts representing various peoples, places, and cultures—certainly food for thought for teachers of early childhood music, with many possibilities for the inclusion of music-related artifacts such as instruments, notated music, costuming worn while performing, photographs of musicians and dancers, and more! The Reggio Emilia philosophy of early childhood learning bears some similarities to the Montessori approach by focusing on the individuality of each child and providing experiences and scaffolds for discovery. Developed by Loris Malaguzzi in Italy, Reggio Emilia encourages young children to express themselves in many different ways (or "languages"), including the arts. Clearly, there are existing music-friendly early childhood education frameworks in place across the globe, providing compelling opportunities to incorporate the world's musical cultures.

Early Childhood Learners: The Basics

In order to educate young children in music and through music so that they might develop cultural respect and understanding, it's necessary to know the children, how they learn, what they know, and what they are capable of learning. Skilled teachers understand the nature of early childhood learners and their developmental characteristics and accept that it is their responsibility to apply age-appropriate instructional techniques that are distinguished from those in use with school-age children in school settings. Young children have different needs and require different kinds of scaffolding than older elementary school children—but it is in these differences that one can find the joy and richness of working within the scope and settings of early childhood learners.

Cognitive Development

Children acquire knowledge rapidly in their early years, such that what they do, and see, and listen to contributes to their impressive cognitive growth prior to the rigors of academic learning in the elementary school. As young children develop cognitively, building knowledge about the world around them from infancy, through toddlerhood, and into the preschool age, the theories of psychologist Jean Piaget are at work and clearly visible (Mooney, 2013). Piaget posited stages of cognitive development that help teachers and caregivers better understand this population. From birth through around 2 years of age, children are in the sensorimotor stage, that is, they learn and develop knowledge through their five senses, seeing, feeling, hearing, smelling, and tasting to make sense of their surroundings. (Many times children in this age span put toys or other objects in their mouths, much to their caregiver's dismay—this, however, is simply part of the learning process.) From 2 years of age through the beginnings of formal schooling, children may be associated with the preoperational stage wherein children see the world as it relates to themselves. Their own experiences are key in the generalization and extrapolation of information. For example, a child may have a dog at home, a familiar four-legged furry friend. When that same child sees a goat at a petting zoo, he may cry out, "dog!" as he is generalizing from his own experience of four-legged creatures. Children in this stage are apt to focus on their own experiences. It is during this phase that many teachers might be mystified as to a child's seemingly off-task contributions, such as abrupt outbursts of information relevant only to the child; for example, "I went to my cousin's birthday party last weekend!" might be exuberantly offered during a preschool circle time discussion of the weather.

As young children learn through personal experiences, observation, immersion, and modeling, it is vital that their early experiences include and address music. In as active a mode as possible, young children need to be doing music—singing, playing, creating it, moving to it in ways that allow them to be fully involved with what the musical world has to offer, in a musical capacity. In many cases, young children do not need a teacher or caregiver to model or facilitate these early experiences with music—they tap into a deep-seated musical instinct to respond, react, and do. Infants, despite their still developing command of linguistic communication, might still use syllables and vocalizations of "ba" or "ma" to show delight with music or attempt to imitate a singing model. Toddlers, newly mobile, might jump into musical expressions of leg bounces and arm flaps, the very beginnings of Eurhythmic movement and dance. Preschoolers bring their rhythmic sense into their playtime, as dolls, trucks, and blocks become musical playthings, tapping on the surrounding floor, walls, and tables. Kindergartners and even first graders, moving toward greater motor skill capacity, might play handclapping games, sing folk songs with friends, or improvise rhythmic utterances while going about the tasks of daily life.

Language and Communication

In the days of infancy (and even before), babies hear the voices and sounds that surround them, even developing preferences for certain vocal and musical timbres. They experiment with communication themselves, babbling, trying on the linguistic (and musical) tasks modeled by their caregivers. The high-pitched, undulating manner of caregivers speaking to babies is highly engaging to them, modeling both speech and music in one behavior. In their early attempts at communicating as infants and even into toddlerhood, they reach and point and imitate modeled sounds. These behaviors give way to the fleshing out of an early vocabulary, stringing words together in short sentences. By the time they are preparing to attend preschool by ages 3 or 4, they are well versed in multiple modes of communication including and beyond the use of spoken language. This includes tone, body language, and facial expression (perhaps to the dismay of caregivers, as "no!" becomes a tool in this communicative arsenal). Typically developing 3- and 4-year-olds can pose questions; structure sentences; demonstrate awareness of syllables, phonemes, and rhymes; and begin to connect spoken sounds with print. By the time pre-Kindergarten, Kindergarten, and first grade enter the picture at ages 4, 5, and 6, children possess and use a vocabulary of several hundred words, recognize written letters, appropriately manipulate books, and engage with printing words and numerals.

The early childhood years represent a time period of great growth in the areas of language and communication. Children may seemingly develop these skills and competencies before our very eyes, and the effective early childhood music teacher can capitalize on their burgeoning communication through an exploration of the world's musical cultures. Songs carry language, and they are effective means of learning language. Consider, for example, the "Mele Pi'āpa," a tune used by Hawaiian children to learn the traditional indigenous language. The tune begins with "There are thirteen letters in the pi'āpa," meaning the Hawaiian alphabet. As the song progresses, children learn the sounds of the various letters, how to incorporate the 'okina (glottal stop) of the Hawaiian language, and how the various diacritical marks are essential to the interpretation and communication of this traditional language.

A glimpse into the musical play of young children of various cultures offers a sense of their penchant for creative vocalizations in speech and song. In her research of the young Miskitu children of Nicaragua, ethnomusicologist Amanda Minks (2013) observed their use of language in musically playful ways, as a prop in the singing of nonsense words, through teasing other children, and in make-believe play. Such linguistic play happens in many cultures, as well as in many preschool settings where young children are stimulated by the sounds they hear not only to learn language but also to invent language, to turn phonemes from verses they do not know into newly expressive chants, rhymes, and rhythms. As young children play and piece together their own languages, why not do the same with the languages of others? As they learn to use their bodies and faces to reflect moods, why not help them understand that music can do the same? As they develop awareness of print and representation of sounds, why not use music as a way to further their awareness? The palette of sounds for musical play grows all the more diverse as young children are exposed to music of the world's cultures.

Physical Development

Again, the swiftness of human development is surely seen in the physical growth that takes place from infancy through the beginning of elementary school. Infants move from a place of total dependency upon a caregiver for mobility, feeding, and comforting, to crawling, scooting, cruising, self-feeding, and the coordination of eyes and hands. Further along the line, toddlers can be found walking, running, climbing, jumping, and throwing, which perhaps might assist them with carrying out a bit of mischief. They can use implements with their hands and respond bodily to music. The pre-Kindergartners and Kindergartners, as well as first graders, demonstrate further skill in locomotor movement, balance, and riding bicycles and scooters and enjoy the challenge of trying out new physical tasks. They show increased skill with drawing, writing, using scissors, and other fine motor skills such as fastening buttons and snaps. These motor skills most certainly transfer into the musical realm, with increasing possibilities for effective use of child-sized musical instruments or manipulatives such as scarves, ribbons, or puppets.

People in many of the world's musical cultures experience music in such a way that music and movement are indistinguishable and inseparable from one another—they combine to form one expressive entity. Young children's affinity for movement provides a wide-open door to exploring the world's music through physical expressiveness and dance. While they may not demonstrate perfect beat keeping or fluid, coordinated motions, their observation and intent are there, along with a willingness and excitement to get up and try moving in a multitude of ways. The development of "musical movement" might look different across cultures. For example, young African American children might find themselves learning the moves and chants associated with handclapping games and double-dutch jump rope, while young children in traditional villages of Quechua-speaking communities in the Andes mountains might begin to observe and attempt the circular dances frequently found in this region. Little ones in Greece, Hungary, and Romania may be introduced to the indigenous folk dances of their culture along with the costuming and celebratory traditions that accompany them. In village life in Malawi and Mozambique, young children dance and sing alongside their parents in various communal gatherings, and when they choose instead to play, they are still rocking and swaying to the sound of live music coming from the village plaza, the church, and the fellowship hall. Young children across the globe are immersed in unique movement traditions that capture their imaginations and facilitate their physical engagement with music.

Social Development

While it might not seem so at first, babies are very social beings! They interact with their caregivers through their giggles, coos, babbles, and cries and use their bodies and faces to initiate contact with others. They come to know the routines of social life and how to demonstrate their needs. As they grow into toddlerhood, young children cultivate relationships with caregivers and can show preferences for familiar caregivers and peers. They are able to follow simple rules and routines, but also might begin to challenge authority. Social play comes into the picture, as does pretend play. Looking ahead into preschool and pre-Kindergarten, and on into Kindergarten and first grade, young children's social and emotional development progress in terms of understanding the self as part of a social group, awareness of themselves as participating in communities with routines and rules, and exploration of social life through play imitative of real-life roles (e.g., playing "house" with a doll). Their development of a sense of self and others manifests through the ability to describe the self and their preferences, associate behavior with consequences, observe different feelings in others, and cooperate with other children in both structured and free play. John Blacking's (1967) classic analysis of children's songs of the Venda culture of South Africa revealed that children's play was most certainly musical in this context, taking on the forms of songs and chants accompanied by various movements. Circle games, hopping, and handstands are other kinesthetic contributions to children's play in this context.

A rise of interest by ethnomusicologists in children's musical cultures reveals that, across the world, even the very young are acquiring music that they hear at home, in daycare and preschool programs, and in the community. The music they receive, whether from nearby or through exposure to music from far-away places, is the music that becomes a part of their musical repertoire. Marisol Berríos-Miranda (2013) wrote of the musical socialization of young children through the influence of family and cultural context across generations in Puerto Rico and the mainland U.S., speaking to the importance of these familial relationships and models in children's musical and social development. The ever-present backdrop of music and the loving encouragement of generations of family members gave rise to a lifelong love of music rooted in early childhood. Beatriz Ilari (2013) highlighted the experiences of young girls growing up on the banks of the Amazon River, using music to explore their social identities, the harshness of their daily realities, and the promise of an empowered future. Lisa Huisman Koops (2013) painted a picture of the musical socialization of children in the African country of Gambia, where children learn very early on to participate fully, and how music might be part of human life in different ways.

It would be unwise to overlook the necessity of these social and emotional competencies in exploring the world's musical cultures. Young children's developing awareness of others has them primed for the experience of diving into the awareness of musical and cultural others. They are naturally curious about the world and the people around them, frequently bombarding their parents and caregivers with the repeated, beseeching inquiry of, "but why?" This natural inquisitiveness is an apt gateway into the many benefits of World Music Pedagogy. Building empathy, demonstrating curiosity, recognizing diversity, and observing others are all part of the process of becoming global musical citizens as well as foundational developmental milestones of early childhood.

Awareness of Diversity and Social Justice

Children are born into a wide diversity of families, places, and spaces, all with different ways of and reasons for engaging with music rooted in cultural practices and personal preferences. A young child might observe early on and then join in making music with a family mariachi band, or observe and then imitate the mediated, digital engagement with music modeled by caregivers, or and listen and then sing the church hymns they know from their weekly visits with family. For some children, singing may be a substantial part of the childhood experience early on, while others may not have models in their lives who are comfortable with that form of musical expression. Children may be enculturated into a system where music and dance are fused into one art form enjoyed by all, while others may learn at an early age that they must sit quietly and watch and listen during live musicking. A song sung to an infant in one corner of the world may be a soothing and calming tune while in other locales may serve to stimulate movement and interaction. Simply put, children are growing and developing in diverse and multifaceted systems and structures in which musical behaviors may look and sound different. They are quite capable of exploring these musical manifestations of their own and others' musical expressions.

In her ethnography of childhood musicking, *Songs in Their Heads*, Patricia Shehan Campbell (2010) highlights these diverse contexts in which young children are first exposed to music making. Among the voices of the many children represented, 6-year-old Ramnad revealed his code-switching between the Indian music of his heritage and the Western Art Music exposure facilitated at school. Lisa, an immigrant to the U.S. from Mexico, retained her love of her homeland through the songs of her heritage and native language. These voices and more reflect the myriad cultural beginnings of children's musical engagement. Five-year-old Darryl's musical life speaks to many things common to early childhood: preference for mediated music, enjoyment of the combination of music and movement, and interest in musical instruments. Carrie, already, by age 6, astutely aware of the musical models in her life, is able to identify with those who choose to sing and those who do not.

If one spends a bit of time observing young children at play, one is certain to, at some point, hear the words, "that's not fair!" Young children are keenly aware of fairness and are quick to observe how opportunities and materials are distributed to themselves and others. Further, young children are acutely aware of difference, frequently having no qualms about pointing out differences in an unfiltered manner. Gender differences, age differences, ethnic differences, and other differences in observable qualities are material for young children to contemplate and discuss. As they notice and articulate difference, they are also observing how their role models deal with (or do not deal with) these important issues, incorporating these attitudes and dispositions into their own interpersonal repertoires.

These natural curiosities present teachers and caregivers with an open doorway into discussions of social justice and diversity. Using child-appropriate language and examples, young children can be easily drawn into discussions of fairness and difference, learning to be open-minded and accepting of others. What better way to engage the issue of fairness and difference than with the incorporation of the world's musical cultures? Through music instruction that contextualizes and humanizes musicking, young children come to know "others" and what makes them special (or even similar). An example might come in the form of a discussion of the musical gender roles in traditional Andean musical cultures. Men traditionally play the instruments (e.g., various flutes) while women serve as singers and lyricists. Many children exclaim, "that's not fair!" in response to acquiring this knowledge. The skillful music teacher must help them understand that the culture enjoys the higher pitched sound of the women's voices, and, as the men cannot sing in that way, they play instruments that mimic that register. What might not seem fair at first glance can be illuminated by a bit of context.

Development of Self and Relationships to Others

Developing a sense of self-concept while cultivating relationships to others is a key aspect of the early childhood years. Young children begin to identify themselves in categorical, observable ways—for instance, "I am a girl" or "I am three years old"—and continue on to more abstract definitions of self as in "I am a good helper" or "My favorite color is green." During this age and stage of early childhood, young children branch out into the development of social relationships as well. They may demonstrate a preference for a particular caregiver or family member. They may begin to develop friendships outside of the family and see other children socially outside of the confines of daycare or school. These early relationships aid in the development of self-concept and social skills, such as, "I am nice to my friends and I can share." Young children also begin to identify as part of larger cultural entities in ethnic, religious, and other capacities, for example, "I am Vietnamese" or "I am Catholic." This is a key time in early childhood development to expose little ones to the various facets of their own and others' cultures, making World Music Pedagogy an appropriate fit for this age group of blossoming musicians.

Musical Development

Alongside and intermixed with these aforementioned important tasks of early childhood development is, of course, musical development. At around 20 weeks of fetal gestation, an unborn child's auditory systems are up and running, allowing him or her to take in the sounds of the mother's environment, perhaps suggesting that musical development begins to blossom before a child emerges into the outside world. As infants, young children develop clear preferences for vocal timbres and can detect musical patterning and experiment with music in various ways as pictured in Figure 1.2. Throughout early childhood, one can observe musical development emerging through movement responses to music, vocal exploration and emergence of singing voice, listening skills, and rhythmic beat competencies. These musical beginnings blossom into capable young musicians who, by first grade, can sing, dance, play child-appropriate instruments, and engage in conversations about the music in their daily lives. Consider the following vignette highlighting these early days of musical development, in which an infant clearly demonstrates her musical preferences and asserts herself in an early childhood music class.

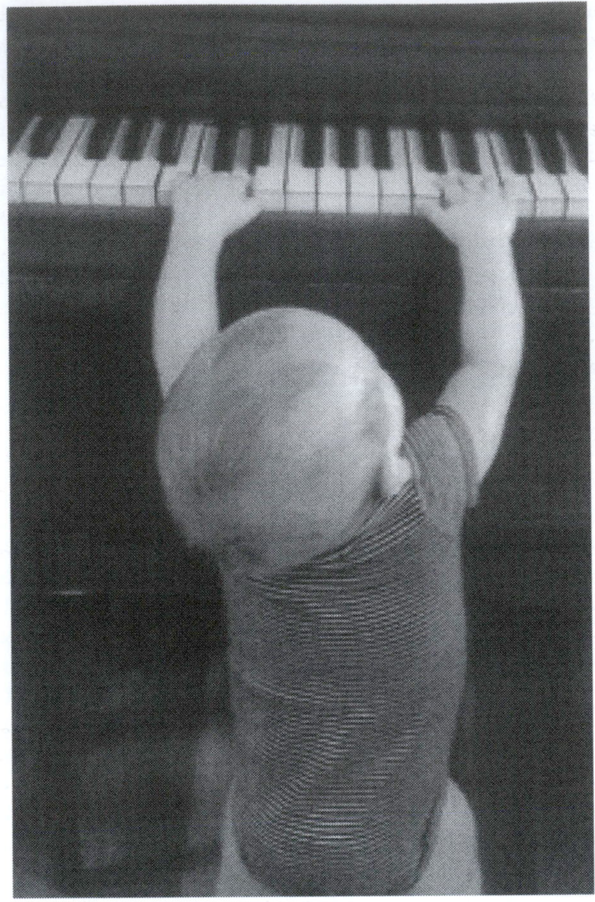

Figure 1.2 Experimenting at the piano

At the Mom & Me Music Class, an array of child-sized instruments is scattered about the floor. There are triangles, hand drums, wood blocks, shakers, tambourines, jingle bells, and other instrument with origins in East Asia, the Middle East, Africa, and Latin America. They are available for the children ages 5 months through 5 years old to experiment with freely before the official start of the facilitated activities. It is a chaotic time, but one in which the children are making meaning in important ways—discovering how to manipulate instruments to create sound, exploring the coordination of movement required to do so, and solidifying preferences for the timbres they like best. In the midst of this pile of instrument choices, baby Maddie never seems quite satisfied with the choices in close proximity to her. Still unable to walk, Maddie scoots on her bottom with purpose across the classroom floor and selects what she has been eyeing—a triangle. Her tiny hands wrap around the silver metal of the instrument and beater, and she makes repeated contact. One day, she may find that the triangle is important to music traditions from 16th century England to contemporary Brazil and Louisiana's Cajun country, but for now she takes pleasure in hearing, seeing, and feeling the cool smooth steel in her grip. Week after week, Maddie does the same thing, scooting from one end of the room to the other to get her hands on the triangle. At less than 1 year of age, she has already developed a preference for the triangle's timbre—and will not let any instrument or person get in the way of playing it!

Intent and Purpose of This Volume

This volume serves as an introduction to the ways and means in which young children can develop musical and cultural knowledge in one fell swoop. It is a coming-to-grips with the unique characteristics of teaching and learning music in the early childhood setting and how these endeavors can and should intersect with purposeful engagement with music of the world's cultures. Young children are tasked with making sense of the world around them, developing identity, and relating to others in pro-social ways. They are quite capable of beginning to understand diversity in humanity, in lifeways and customs, and in art forms, including music, making the early childhood years a fertile time to introduce a multiplicity of sounds and contexts. Those involved with early childhood music are tasked with acknowledging and celebrating the diversity of children in order to provide encounters from locally living and global communities, and they are wise to possibilities for young children's meaningful reflection of their own and other cultures (and their musical sounds).

Early childhood learners may span the ages of birth through 8 years old—this volume will give special attention to the range between the ages of 2 and 7 years, including children in nurseries, daycare settings, preschools, Kindergarten, and the very beginnings of first grade. World Music Pedagogy makes strategic use of listening, discussion, movement, and creativity—while infant and toddler musical engagement is most certainly vital, the approach that is most appropriate for those very early years may not be entirely compatible with the various facets of the formal application World Music Pedagogy. Rather, the very youngest music learners may be exposed to the world's musical cultures through hearing singing models, live instrumental music, or recorded music (without specific directions to respond).

Chapter 1 assists the teacher in developing an awareness of the unique aspects of this age and stage of childhood as well as an overview of the process of engaging young children, specifically, in age-appropriate World Music Pedagogy encounters. This age group requires teachers to possess and make application of a deep knowledge of early childhood development, music pedagogy, and the social, cultural, and contextual issues associated with engaging with the world's musical cultures.

Chapter 2 offers an exploration of implementation of the first step in the World Music Pedagogy process, Attentive Listening activities for young children in which they are listening for and to the elements of music in child-friendly ways. Attentive Listening activities for this age group might include practical applications of listening maps and manipulatives such as finger puppets, child-sized instruments, felt board pieces, scarves, ribbons, and even everyday objects found around the home. Various manipulatives in the Attentive Listening stage provide child-friendly and concrete ways of exploring music. For example, children might use a scarf to explore space and respond to the expressive qualities of the music they hear. A finger puppet could be a friendly helper in engaging the voice in different ways or following along with melodic contour.

Chapter 3 offers participatory pathways to the next stages of the World Music Pedagogy process, Engaged Listening and Enactive Listening. Engaged Listening invites children to become involved musically in some capacity as they listen to a performance or recording of world music. Enactive Listening takes the listening even further as children move into the performance of these musical excerpts in contextually appropriate ways. Ideas for age-appropriate active music making involving singing, movement, instrumental performance, and more are presented. Music is social and music is for doing—even for little ones. Children in the early childhood setting are natural participators in music, and this chapter presents ways to engage them in what they love to do.

Chapter 4 focuses on performance of the world's musical cultures and explores the ways in which early childhood music learners may showcase their musical and cultural encounters through public performance. Public sharing of the world's musical cultures may occur in informal ways through the hosting of classroom visitors or even in more formal contexts in the performance of a short piece in a school-wide concert. Many activities can even be combined to craft a short pageant featuring the children's musical products through song, speech, and movement.

Chapter 5 investigates age-appropriate applications of composition and improvisation for early childhood learners making use of the voice, movement, and instruments. In Creating World Music, a case is made for the importance of offering opportunities for young children to make their own music, developing ideas that spill over from the earlier experiences they have had as listeners, singers, dancers, and players. From the very beginning of engaging their voices, young children are improvising babbles and sounds and songs. From age 4 and beyond, they may more systematically engage that improvisatory nature through the creation of rhythmic patterns and ostinati, song lyrics, Eurhythmic movements, or instrumental soundscapes using barred percussion and unpitched percussion instruments.

Chapter 6 focuses on cross-curricular integrations and features ideas for aiding young children in making connections between musics of the world and their own lives, cultures, communities, and beyond. Music adeptly serves as the intersection between children's lives and exploration of the facets of the world such as cultural customs, daily family life, stories, places, and sounds. A major task of children in the early years of life is to begin to form an identity while making sense of the world around them. Music can and should be an integral part of this meaning making.

Chapter 7 concludes the volume by assessing the challenges and outcomes inherent in engaging young children in the World Music Pedagogy process, understanding the early childhood music learner as well as music as a part of identity formation in personal and cultural ways. While early childhood learners may not be considered a "clean slate," their "newness" to the world offers a unique and poignant opportunity to use music as the vehicle for understanding the interconnectedness of humanity and the unique roles they may play within it.

As mentioned in the foreword, the reader will find episodes with ready-made procedures to facilitate the various components of the World Music Pedagogy process with early childhood music learners. Some are intended to highlight just one aspect of the process, while three Learning Pathways see the reader through all aspects of the World Music Pedagogy process. These three Learning Pathways invite teachers and children to more deeply explore music of indigenous Hawai'i, China, and West Africa.

It should be noted that this volume may be useful to a variety of stakeholders in the world of early childhood education. While the most immediately obvious applications might appeal to teachers of music, others, such as early childhood classroom teachers, caregivers, and parents, can most certainly make use of the information and ideas presented here. Early childhood classroom teachers can incorporate a musical activity into a morning circle time gathering or combine musicking with the study of a particular region of the world. Parents and caregivers may bring active listening and musicking into the home, even using the ideas within this volume as a point of departure for more deeply exploring family genealogy and culture. Any individual involved in cultivating curious, open-minded, and musical children may benefit from applying the tenets of World Music Pedagogy.

Starting the Journey

Early childhood is a developmental period ripe with musical curiosity and excitement (Figure 1.3). To engage early childhood learners in the world's musical cultures is to open a treasure chest of developmental potentials and cultural awakenings. Through efforts to design and deliver experiences based upon the dimensions of World Music Pedagogy, young children are cultivating the various domains of their cognitive, physical, social, and emotional learning while fostering the tools and skills necessary to be diversity-focused

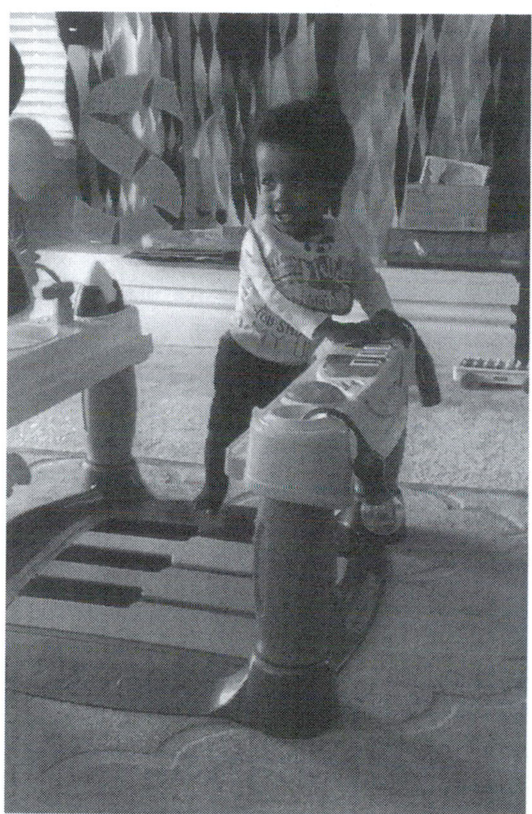

Figure 1.3 Very busy making music!

musical citizens of the world. The possibilities are rich for bringing young children into an awareness of their world through music; read on to start the journey!

References

Blacking, J. (1967). *Venda children's songs: A study in ethnomusicological analysis*. Chicago, IL: The University of Chicago Press.

Burns, S. (2017). *Music education through a Montessori lens: Every child has musical potential*. Retrieved from https://nafme.org/music-education-montessori-lens-every-child-musical-potential/

Berríos-Miranda, M. (2013). Musical childhoods across three generations from Puerto Rico to the USA. In P. S. Campbell and T. Wiggins (Eds.), *The Oxford handbook of children's musical cultures* (301–324). New York, NY: Oxford University Press.

Campbell, P. S. (2004). *Teaching music globally*. New York, NY: Oxford University Press.

Campbell, P. S. (2010). *Songs in their heads: Music and its meaning in children's lives* (2nd Ed.). New York, NY: Oxford University Press.

Ilari, B. (2013). Musical cultures of girls in the Brazilian Amazon. In P. S. Campbell and T. Wiggins (Eds.), *The Oxford handbook of children's musical cultures* (131–146). New York, NY: Oxford University Press.

Koops, L. H. (2013). Enjoyment and socialization in Gambian children's music making. In P. S. Campbell and T. Wiggins (Eds.), *The Oxford handbook of children's musical cultures* (266–281). New York, NY: Oxford University Press.

Minks, A. (2013). *Voices of play: Miskitu children's speech and song on the Atlantic coast of Nicaragua*. Tucson, AZ: The University of Arizona Press.

Mooney, C. G. (2013). *Theories of childhood* (2nd Ed.). St. Paul, MN: Redleaf Press.

2

Attentive Listening for Cultural Awakenings

In the brightly lit, blue-carpeted all-purpose room of the daycare, the preschool music class comes to a close. Bubbly 4-year-olds carefully examine the stamps inked onto their hands as a reward for their hard work (and play). Miss Mary, the music teacher, begins to pack up the many items that had made the morning magical: a guitar, egg shakers, sheer scarves for dancing, puppets, a felt board, and even an ocean drum for sharing. Thirty solid minutes of joyful musicking covered everything from vocal exploration, to singing familiar folk tunes from European and African American traditions, to building movement vocabulary, to playing instruments both as individuals and an ensemble and even exploring where their musical repertoires came from, relating to the people and places that give rise to musical expressions. Non-musical objectives were also covered, important aspects of learning in the early childhood setting such as sharing, taking turns, moving safely about the room, and speaking kind words to one another.

The class is over, but one more lesson is yet to be learned—by Miss Mary. In the midst of the colorful chaos of cleaning up, a tiny hand is thrust into the air. This tiny hand belongs to a little one with a cherubic face who earnestly exclaims, "But we didn't do any real *music today!" A bit baffled, Miss Mary stands back and thinks for a moment, mystified at this assessment given the wall-to-wall music making that had just occurred.*

An afternoon's contemplation reveals to Miss Mary the reasoning behind this preschooler's seemingly misplaced comment—the day's music class had not included any recorded musical selections for listening! It becomes clear in that moment the extent to which young children value the experience of hearing "real" music, of being immersed in sounds both new and familiar, that come from the voices and instruments of professional musicians. Contemporary young children have an unprecedented level of access to recorded music, a level perhaps not known or enjoyed by the generation of their parents and teachers, and a surprising level of sophistication, which allows them to recognize, if only through their enthusiastic responses, the sounds of quality musicians, both live and on recordings. Young children are media savvy and capable—they access music through their home television sets, through DVDs and CDs of music both marketed for children and those which are enjoyed by the adults in their lives, and through computers, tablets, phones, toys, and more. It makes sense, then, for Miss Mary to indulge the request of this little one and to harness children's interest in recorded music, using this vehicle as a path to musical and cultural awakenings. So, she is ready to infuse into her work with children a compilation of recordings that feature Mexican mariachi, Hawaiian hula, Jewish klezmer, stringed instruments from China, and Navajo social dance songs.

Attentive Listening

The first phase of the process of World Music Pedagogy invites young children to engage in Attentive Listening, which is intended pedagogically as a thoughtful and intentional way of inviting little ones to listen to the features of the music, such as instrumentation, dynamics, timbre, mood, or styles of articulations (smooth, separated, etc.). This they can do well, provided that the teacher selects the music carefully and provides the sorts of questioning that fits their capacity to focus their attention on discrete components of music. Additionally, teachers should be advised that short excerpts are best for these listening encounters, 30 to 45 seconds being an ideal span of time. Particularly from age 3 years and onward, young children can be drawn into the midst of musical recordings through questions that develop their sense of awe and curiosity in what the music contains and communicates to them. This first phase of musical discovery may also include some type of listening map or visual, a simple gesture or free movement, something to help young learners grasp the intangible aspects of music. Children might be invited to pat a beat that matches the meter of a piece of music, clue in to timbres by using descriptive words such as "scratchy" and "smooth," or use a finger to draw a melodic contour in the air as it ascends, descends, wiggles around, or is sustained on a single pitch.

Listening to Learn: A Pedagogical Priority

The developmental tasks of early childhood are significant and demanding. Developing fine and gross motor skills, learning to be independent in feeding and dressing, cultivating academic skills of reading, writing, and language usage, exploring social life through family relationships and friendships—these and more occupy these early learners as they begin to make sense of the world around them.

To ignore the role of listening in the development of young children would be short-sighted. Even from the final few months of their pre-natal days, infants are hearing the sounds of their mother's world, the voices and music of her surrounds. They enter the world ready to hear and use that information to develop a sense of their environments. They apply this sense to interpret tone and feelings, to recognize their caregivers, and to begin developing language skills. It is this sense of hearing that facilitates the imitation and eventually acquisition of spoken language.

One must not make the error, however, of conflating hearing and listening. While "hearing" may connote a physiological phenomenon of sound waves entering the ear canal and stimulating the precise inner workings of the ear, the term "listening" carries with it a larger burden, and also greater splendors, for the giving of attention brings the gifts of discovering aural treasures. Listening entails the direction of attention to the sound source, whether that is a human voice, birds chirping in trees, the honking of car horns, or musical instruments being performed. Beyond that, listening implies an analysis of the sound source—is this sound communicating a warning of danger? Or is this a pleasant sound that is meant to be enjoyed? Do I like this sound? Why? How can I describe what the sound means to me, and how does that compare to the performer? This last question is a cultural awakening, in that children are finding their own feelings for sound, and are learning to think about sound, even as they take the first steps in recognizing that their own feelings may compare or contrast with those of people from another place in the world.

With young children born into the world as natural listeners, it seems unfortunate, then, that more purposeful listening is not taking place in the places and spaces of children's learning, both in the home and in educational settings. Far too often, music is simply left to the background of children's lives, a silly song to accompany a cartoon program, the parents' choice of music played in family car rides, the ever-present soothing classical soundscape of the daycare center nap time. Children listen with purpose, and the individuals responsible for caring for and teaching these little ones are responsible for teaching them to cultivate that natural instinct.

Perhaps the role of listening in daily life is broadly underestimated, but especially so in the early childhood years. Listening to music with focus and purpose not only cultivates the skill of interacting with music in that way, but fosters listening skills that can transfer to various aspects of their educational, social, and professional lives. Listening with purpose must occur in the school setting as new concepts are introduced and practiced. Listening with purpose must occur in social relationships, developing interpersonal intelligences and the caring relatedness sought after by humans. Listening with purpose must occur in the workplace, ensuring the understanding of directives and effective communication with colleagues. There is no better time and place to start listening than in the early childhood years.

Take, for example, Episode 2.1, that whisks children away to Hawai'i and draws them into the world of *hula*, an ancient art form of storytelling through movement. In the early days of the Hawaiian kingdom, their language was strictly of an aural-oral tradition. In order to preserve the many important myths, legends, genealogies, and treasure troves of cultural information, hula was used as an artistic aid in the memorization and transmission of culture. "Anoai" is a *hula kahiko*, or ancient hula, accompanied by the *'uli 'uli*, gourd rattles adorned with feathers. Figure 2.1 depicts a photograph of the *'uli 'uli* gourd rattles with yellow and red feathers, the colors frequently found as instrument adornments due to their association with the *Ali'i*, or Hawaiian royalty. Feathers of these hues were challenging to procure and were reserved for the highest of rank.

The story of "Anoai" is multi-layered, telling first of the light rain falling on the lehua blossoms, but more deeply telling of the story of Hopoe, one of the ancient practitioners and teachers of hula who favored the lehua blossom. It should be noted that the ancient hulas are described "chanted" rather than "sung," despite the

Figure 2.1 *'Uli 'uli* Hawaiian gourd rattles

similarities in the vocal production of sounds. In this episode, teachers may invite children to consider the instruments they hear and how these might help tell a story about something familiar, orienting young children to the typical timbres, both instrumental and vocal, found within the ancient world of hula. It provides something for every young child (and certainly not those of Pacific Islander experience alone): how rain is illustrated musically by an instrument with which they may have familiarity, at least by way of rattles they have known in their infancy, and how a voice may convey expressions within a very small range of pitches. Further encounters with this Learning Pathway piece will extend young children's involvement with this hula mele.

Episode 2.1: Lehua Blossoms in the Rain: Hawaiian Musical Storytelling (Learning Pathway #1)

(For Attentive Listening)

Specific Use: Ages 3 to 6

Materials:

- "Anoai," Jacob Feuerring with Tom Hiona, Smithsonian Folkways, photograph of lehua blossom, set of *'uli 'uli* or photograph, egg shakers

Procedure:

1. "This piece of music is about something that happens with the weather. Listen and try to figure out what type of weather this might be about."
2. Play track.
3. Discuss answers (rain).
4. "You heard an instrument called the *'uli 'uli*. It is a type of shaker made from a gourd and has different colors of feathers on the top. The sound of the *'uli 'uli* might make us think of little rain drops falling down."
5. Show photographs of *'uli 'uli* or the real instruments.
6. "Listen again and tell me if you hear another kind of instrument."
7. Play track.
8. Discuss answers (voice).
9. "Yes! Your voice is a kind of musical instrument that is inside your own body. You might be surprised to know that in Hawai'i they say this voice is a 'chanting' voice instead of a 'singing' voice. Can you listen again to this chanting voice and see what else you can tell me about the person?"
10. Play track.
11. Discuss answers (chanter has a man's voice, is a grown-up, answers will vary).
12. "Listen one last time and use your fingertips to show the sounds of the rain."
13. Play track.

An opportunity to listen calmly and with focus comes with the Learning Pathway in Episode 2.2, "Moli Hua," a Chinese children's song. From the 18th century, this popular tune known by many Chinese children tells of the jasmine flower, a blossom that opens at night and closes its petals at the arrival of daylight. In fact, it was one of the first Chinese folk songs to gain popularity outside of China. While some translations and iterations of the song tell of plucking jasmine blossoms to share, some warn against picking a flower for fear of a scolding from the gardener. This tune has found many popular and political applications from Summer Olympic opening ceremony music to symbols of resistance movements. "Moli Hua" is a pentatonic tune and has been arranged into many different forms from the a cappella strains of children's voices to the choral arrangement featured here. This gentle melody provides children and teachers with the opportunity to consider mood and style in music and how musicians may approach their craft in ways that elicit certain feelings from listeners. While this piece of music does have text, children may be invited to listen and ponder how the sounds invite one to consider the characteristics of fragile flower petals.

Episode 2.2: The Gentle Jasmine: A Chinese Melody (Learning Pathway #2)

(For Attentive Listening)

Specific Use: Ages 3 to 6

Materials:

- "Moli Hua," Crystal Children's Choir & Karl Chang, iTunes, photograph of jasmine flower/vine, sun and moon visuals, scarves/ribbons for dancing

Procedure:

1. "Listen to my piece of music and tell me if this is a very gentle piece of music or a very fast, exciting piece."
2. Play track.
3. Discuss answers (gentle).
4. Listen again and see what you can tell me about this music that sounds gentle to you."
5. Discuss answers (tempo, timbre, dynamic level).
6. "This is a Chinese song about a flower called a jasmine blossom. Flowers are fragile, so it makes sense that this is a gentle piece of music."
7. "Listen again and try to do a two-finger tap to the sounds of the singers' voices."
8. Play track.
9. Observe/assess tapping to melodic contour.

The following Learning Pathway in Episode 2.3 invites children to consider the interesting timbres of the West African xylophone, with its many layers of rhythm and melodic material. This music originates in the West African nation of Nigeria, specifically featuring the ethnic group of the Tera People. A peace-loving people, the Tera tribe rarely use the xylophone as a solo instrument, despite what the recording features. Players of the xylophone play only—they do not sing along as might be found in other culture groups. While listening to the Tera xylophone (also called "*shinji*"), teachers and children may take on the task of finding and maintaining a steady beat by tapping or patting. For those unaccustomed to the rhythmic complexities of music of this region of the world, the beat keeping task might present a challenge to younger children. Children may also be engaged by the unique timbres of this instrument, giving careful consideration to where it might come from and what it might look like (see Figure 2.2).

Episode 2.3: X Marks the Spot: Xylophones of West Africa (Learning Pathway #3)

(For Attentive Listening)

Specific Use: Ages 5 to 7

Materials:

- "Tera Xylophone," Music from the Villages of Northeastern Nigeria, Smithsonian Folkways, photograph of West African xylophone

Procedure:

1. "Listen to my piece of music and try to figure out what kind of instrument you are hearing."
2. Play track.
3. Discuss answers (xylophone).
4. "Listen again and see if you can tell me how many people are playing together."
5. Play track.
6. Discuss answers (one, although it might sound like more!)
7. "Where in the world do you think this xylophone comes from? Listen and try to figure it out!"
8. Discuss answers (West Africa, Nigeria)
9. "Listen one last time and try to pat a steady beat to the music."
10. Play track.
11. Observe/assess beat keeping.

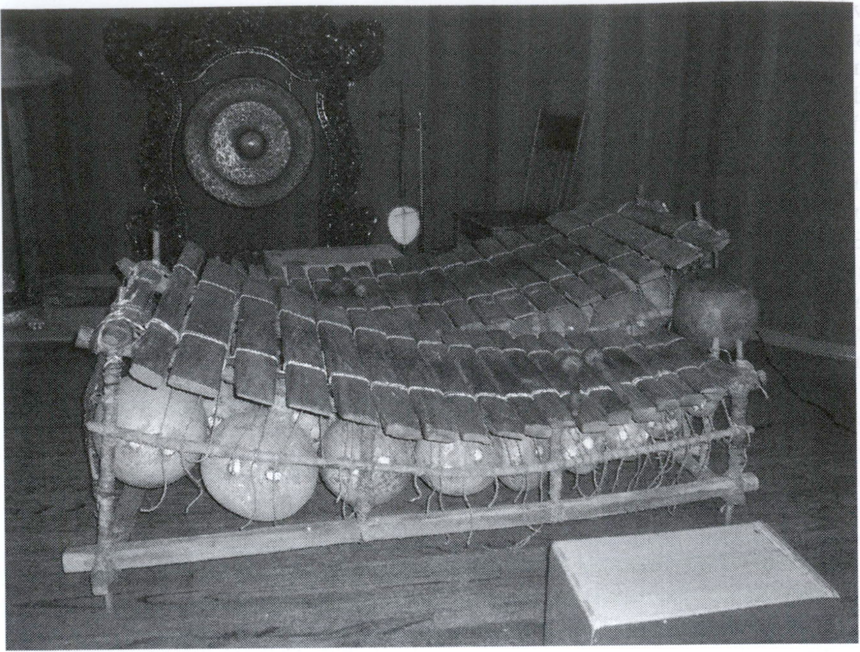

Figure 2.2 West African xylophones

Listening as Gateway to Cultural Understanding

As young children are instinctively wired for listening, it makes sense, then, to tap into this natural compulsion in order to cultivate musical knowledge. They are perfectly capable of listening intelligently for various musical concepts and expressive features—they may not fully realize they are doing so, but instinctively sense and feel these in their brains and bodies. Young children may demonstrate their interpretations of these musical concepts through vocalizations and movements. They are naturally musical and uninhibited in their expressions of delight in responding to music.

A compelling aspect of the early childhood developmental years, music is an ideal pathway for inviting young children to consider the world around them both locally and globally. They are naturally curious about the primary aspects involved in creating music—people and sound—a great way to open the door to rooting their music listening in culture.

Anyone who has interacted with young children is likely to understand their need to share and relate. Many a lesson or morning circle time has been derailed by stories of a cousin's birthday party or a family pet's recent bath or pointing out that the student and teacher are both wearing the same color. This compulsion to share and relate is frequently demonstrated in their music learning, as well. For example, in learning about the often enormous *taiko* drums of Japan, it is not uncommon for a child to joyfully squeal that she has Japanese heritage. Upon learning about the sounds of the mariachis of Mexico, a little one might interject that he visited Mexico with his family. Hearing the songs, games, and chants of Ghanaian children might spark the outburst of "I play games like that, too!" Young children often demonstrate more facility in quickly making connections to the world's musical cultures than their adult counterparts. Their desire for relatedness and sense of wonder are powerful tools in open and accepting listening.

While the previous lesson episodes start young children on the Learning Pathways through the entire World Music Pedagogy process, there are many ways to incorporate the world's musical cultures into short-term Attentive Listening encounters. Episode 2.4 invites children to travel to southeast Asia to the country of Vietnam, so filled with color, culture, activity, sights, smells, and friendly faces. "Con Voi" translates to "baby elephant"—while many children may not have seen a real live elephant in person, they can certainly relate to the more concrete notion of imagining a large animal stomping and lumbering about. "Con Voi" was recorded by the Vietnamese National Song and Dance Ensemble, founded in 1952 during wartime conflict with France. Originally founded to bring music and dance to soldiers and villagers, this ensemble has dedicated itself to the collection and preservation of traditional songs and stories of the various ethnic minorities of Vietnam. Based in the city of Hanoi, this group of musicians and dancers makes use of unique blends of traditional Vietnamese and Western musical instruments, as well as interesting orchestrations and musical textures. (See Figure 2.3 for a glimpse into a traditional

Figure 2.3 A glimpse of a Vietnamese traditional instrument shop

Vietnamese instrument shop.) Teachers may use this episode to help young children apply their listening skills to understand how music may, through timbre, tempo, and articulation, bring about the imagery of something entirely non-musical—like an elephant stomping about!

Episode 2.4: Here Come the Elephants! Trunks, Tails, and Toes in Vietnam

(For Attentive Listening)

Specific Use: Ages 4 to 6

Materials:

- "Con Voi," Vietnamese National Song and Dance Ensemble, Smithsonian Folkways, elephant finger puppets (optional)

Procedure:

1. "Music friends, please listen to my piece of music and tell me which animal you think it could be about."
2. Play track.
3. Discuss answers (will vary).
4. "This piece of music is about an elephant! Is an elephant big or small?"
5. Discuss answers.
6. "Please listen again and tell me what you hear that makes this music sound like an elephant."
7. Play track.
8. "Listen again and show me the big giant elephant steps with your hands in your lap."
9. Play track.
10. (Optional) Extend the activity by distributing elephant finger puppets (pictured in Figure 2.4) and inviting children to move the manipulatives about the room in an elephant-like fashion. Stomp to the drum beats and string bass down bows.

Teachers may wish to follow up with the children, connecting the low timbre, broad articulation, and lumbering tempo with the hulking frame of the elephant. Assisting children in moving from their own descriptions of these musical concepts into usage of the academic terms may come about from engagement in this episode.

Everything is big in the world of a preschooler! The following encounter in Episode 2.5 asks children to consider the sounds of drums and just how big they can be

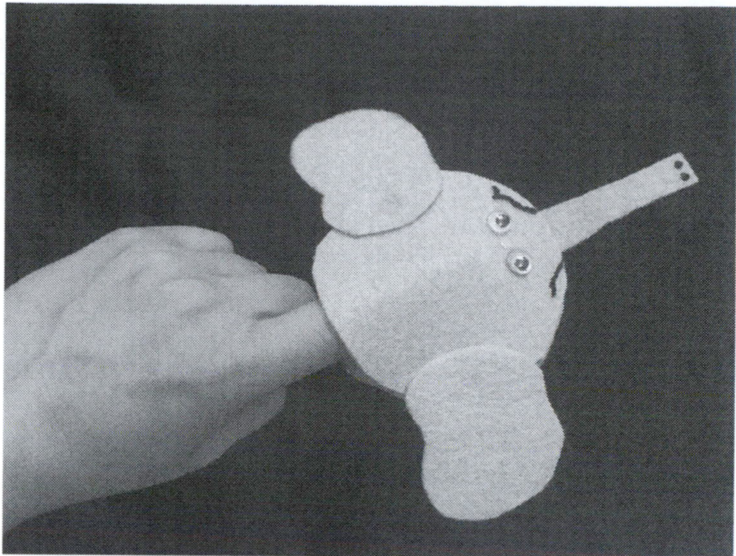

Figure 2.4 Elephant finger puppet manipulative

in the realm of Japanese *taiko* drumming, an ancient musical tradition that includes far more than just drums, factoring movement and technique into playing, almost akin to a form of martial arts. Instruments may range in size from a typical Western snare drum to as large as a vehicle! Attitude, approach, and energy are important in this art form, with relationships cultivated between performer and instrument. *Taiko* has an extensive history with many uses in theater, warfare, and other cultural applications. Bringing a large gathering drum or bass drum into the music lesson might help young children conceptualize and relate to the instruments found in a *taiko* ensemble. Feeling the vibrations of a very large drum can help little ones more aptly grasp the science behind the sounds of these drums. As soon as young children hear a drum, their instinct to imitate drumming motions takes over and they tap away!

Episode 2.5: Go Big or Go Home: *Taiko* Drums of Japan

(For Attentive Listening)

Specific Use: Ages 3 to 6

Materials:

- "Taiko Drumming," Taiko Drums: Music of Japan, iTunes, photo of *taiko* drum and player

Procedure:

1. "Please listen to my piece of music and tell me what kind of instrument you hear."
2. Play track.
3. Discuss answers (drum).
4. "Yes, you are hearing drums! Please listen again and tell me if you think you hear big, giant drums or tiny, little drums."
5. Play track.
6. Discuss answers (big drums).
7. "Listen again and tell me, what was your hint that you were hearing big drums?"
8. Play track.
9. "There are all kinds of drums in the world, some very small and some very, very big! These big drums are called *taiko* drums, and they come from Japan. Can you imagine playing an instrument that is as big as you?"
10. Extend this encounter by showing a photograph of a *taiko* drum in relation to the size of the person playing the drum and by allowing children to play a large gathering drum for comparative purposes.

Young Children's Listening Responses

Observing young children in the act of careful listening can be quite informative in terms of how they are perceiving the various musical features they are hearing. For example, Kindergarteners engaged in careful listening might do so with a focus object or manipulative in their hands, such as a silicone circle, scarf, or finger puppet. They frequently use their manipulatives to demonstrate what they hear—choppy movements when they hear staccato music; smooth and flowing movements when they hear something legato; large, grand movements for forte, stately selections; small movements for something very soft; and all the things in between. Young children sense these musical features and respond in natural ways—they frequently do not even need to be instructed to respond to the many and varied expressive qualities they may hear.

Choosing music for young children's careful and purposeful listening is a skillful endeavor. In addition to a wide variety of world cultures, teachers and caregivers must consider variety in timbre, tempo, dynamics, articulation, meter, mode, style, historical context, and more. Young children are naturally drawn to the "groovy" nature of traditional Andean music, the bright and festive sounds of Caribbean music, the booming drum beats of Japanese *taiko*, the vocables of indigenous musics of North America, the syrupy swoops of Hawaiian slack key guitar, and more. They most certainly develop particular preferences, as well, and their own personal favorites! Consider the case of the 6-month-old baby in an immersive music class who observed all activities quietly until Beethoven was played—he responded with vigorous bobs of the head, flapping of his tiny arms, and scooting of his legs and feet!

Teachers know and understand the complexities of programmatic musical works with layers of imagery, narrative, or symbolism ascribed to musical sound. A challenge for teachers, then, might be to make these programmatic selections relatable to children, providing them with a doorway in to make meaning of multifaceted works for themselves. As in the Vietnamese selection, "Con Voi," "El Jilguerillo," a mariachi tune, tells of an animal friend that can be relatable to children: the black and yellow bird, the goldfinch. Mariachi as a musical genre originated in Mexico and is widely embraced by Mexicans abroad as emblematic of their identity. The form of mariachi enjoyed today had its origins in Jalisco. The typical mariachi ensemble is a unique blend of European and Mexican influences and includes trumpets, violins, guitarrón, vihuela, and guitar. While some of these instruments remain in their original European forms, others, such as the guitarrón and vihuela, represent instruments of Mexican origin. Mariachi is known for its lively and sometimes syncopated rhythms, as well as for the brilliance and virtuosity of its instruments' performance techniques. "El Jilguerillo" is a *son*, one of the variety of musical genres performed by mariachis. *Son* as a genre represents influences from Mexico, Spain, and Africa and varies from region to region. The *son* featured in Episode 2.6 tells not just of the little goldfinch, but beckons the bird to carry a love letter to one who is missed. This episode engages young children in multiple ways, inviting them to relate the sounds they hear to the possibilities of animals that could be represented by those sounds. Further, children may give consideration to the mood of the piece, wondering if it is happy or sad, eventually learning that there is a hint of melancholy to the story of "El Jilguerillo" and even making connections to the happy and sad soundtracks of their own lives. Children may delight in the instrument pretend play and goldfinch movement activities, as well.

Episode 2.6: Feathered Friends and Magnificent Mariachi

(For Attentive Listening)

Specific Use: Ages 4 to 6

Materials:

- "El Jilguerillo," Nati Cano's Mariachi Los Camperos, Smithsonian Folkways

Procedure:

1. "Please listen to my music and tell what animal you think this might be about."
2. Play track.
3. Discuss answers.
4. "You may be surprised to find out this song is about a kind of bird called a goldfinch. It is a bright yellow bird with black marks on its wings and a black cap. Listen again to my song and tell me what parts might sound like a bird."
5. Discuss answers.
6. "Please listen and tell me if you think this is a happy song or a sad song. Why?"

7. Play track.
8. Discuss answers (will vary based on personal experience).
9. "This song is played by a kind of band called 'mariachi.' This song might sound kind of happy but is really about missing someone very much. What music would you listen to when you miss someone?"
10. Discuss answers.
11. "Listen carefully and see if you can tell me some of the instruments that are part of the mariachi band. You may pretend play the instrument of your choice."
12. Play track.
13. Discuss answers (violins, trumpets, guitars, vihuela, guitarrón).
14. "Listen one last time and tell me your favorite of these instruments you hear. You may move your hands and arms like a little goldfinch while you are listening."
15. Play track.
16. Discuss answers.

Deep Listening for Cultural Awakenings

A typical early childhood music class is a high-energy affair, featuring singing, movement, storytelling, dancing, rhythmic chants, props and manipulatives, instruments, and, of course, listening. In these early days of music instruction, when children are eager to please, it can be most fascinating to engage them in age-appropriate discussions of the nuts and bolts of music. They frequently have far more profound things to say than teachers might assume. For example, during a rowdy class entrance, a Kindergartner noted, "We should really be more *piano*," inferring that he had not only the capacity to distinguish a dynamic level, but was using vocabulary from an earlier learning experience. Young children crave the insider knowledge of music and to be able to share and discuss. The topic of listening, then, can and should be part of these discussions.

The daily life of a teacher is hectic, for sure, a jam-packed existence filled with lesson planning and preparation, assessment, performances, professional development, and communication with parents and colleagues, along with a few occasional stolen moments of respite. This existence can be even more overcrowded for the itinerant teacher who may take on the responsibilities of teaching in multiple childcare centers during the day, unpacking and repacking materials several times per day, and fighting traffic to arrive at the next class on time. In this whirlwind of activity, it can be tempting to treat listening encounters as a moment to drop focus, to prepare materials while children are listening, or to clean up from a prior activity. The teacher should be cautioned, however, that her behavior is being observed just as closely as the music itself. In order to cultivate deep listening, teachers must model deep listening themselves, with a quiet body and careful attention.

Adults have their own approaches to musical listening, developing preferences, pursuing access to music in live or mediated formats. Young children may perform many of the same tasks, cultivating their own preferences, their own sounds and songs to which they are drawn. Children, however, are not tiny adults. Their contact with music is limited to what they can access in their environments, what is provided by their caregivers, whereas an adult can have a far wider reach in indulging their listening. These limitations are not always limiting, though. Take, for example, the following, which demonstrates the ways in which a child uses what is in his environment to determine listening choices.

Three-year-old AJ loves music. His tiny electronic keyboard is a remnant from his parents' childhood, but that does not stop him from engaging with this instrument as if it were thoroughly modern and new. He is adept at making sure the keyboard is plugged in, frequently moving it from room to room in his home. More frequently than playing the keys in a melodic sort of way, AJ is drawn to the pre-set musical features. His top two choices vacillate between an electronic-sounding samba beat and a full-blown electro-arrangement of "Wake Me Up Before You Go-Go" by the 1980s band Wham!. These sounds elicit a series of high-energy dance maneuvers featuring jumps, spins, and crashing into the sofa. When AJ is heavily immersed in his keyboard sessions, he can frequently be seen dashing into the home office and emerging with a cloth storage box of musical instruments, including a soprano recorder, shakers, rhythm sticks, and a rainbow-colored child-sized glockenspiel. While the tones, timbres, and rhythms might not go together in the world of adults trained in music, in AJ's world, they make perfect sense.

Young Children and Music: Mediated and Live Access

Children's access to mediated music has been facilitated by the advent of tablets, smart phones, television streaming services, and other technological devices. At very young ages, children can deftly manipulate these devices and make choices about the sounds they are hearing, whether these are musical sounds or the various sonic bits of cartoons and interactive games. One might posit that this personal engagement with sound and high level of choice and control could speak to a need for communal listening and listening encounters where the child does not always make the choice. Listening together is social, communal, taking place in the varied spaces in which life happens: the home, the car, stores and restaurants, religious rituals, community events, or sports. Children are immersed in these communal listening experiences—Attentive Listening gives them the opportunity to be more present in their listening.

Becoming more present in listening encounters can be assisted by live listening experiences. Children are naturally drawn to instruments, how they work, how they are played, how they produce their different sounds. Early childhood listeners are capable of listening to live music mindfully and crafting responses meaningful to their lives and contexts. Upon hearing a live demonstration of a Western Boehm-system flute, a little one thoughtfully and serenely offered, "That sounds like a baby duck trying to quack." While the flutist herself might have described her tone and technique differently, the child made many careful observations and applications—the sound is high and probably matches with something small, a baby animal, perhaps. What kinds of baby animals make sounds? Baby ducks!

Typically developing children are closely attuned to mood—how their caregivers are feeling, how facial expressions and body language can communicate emotions. The following episode presents children with the opportunity to listen carefully and match music and mood using a chart of illustrated faces that show varying emotions. The Barefoot Natives, a Hawaiian music duo featuring the talents of Uncle Willie K and Eric Gilliom, perform a repertoire of uplifting and compelling music, including "E Komo Mai," the Hawaiian term for "welcome." This song of welcome is upbeat, inspires movement and smiles, and provides a doorway in to exploring mood and music through Attentive Listening. When working with music of the world's cultures, teachers may initially be drawn to the ancient or traditional songs and chants that have stood the test of time. It is important, however, to demonstrate to children that musical practices the world over still grow, develop, adapt, and mutate over time. "E Komo Mai" in Episode 2.7 presents a wonderful opportunity to show children that contemporary musicians draw from their traditional sound worlds and create new and special ways of musicking. Further, this episode presents an opportunity to consider interpersonal skills and social intelligences through music. A poster of emotion faces sets the stage for young children's listening, inviting them to consider the ways in which the body can show feelings and share information. This concept is key in the Hawaiian culture as hula meles for centuries have used the body and the face to communicate.

Episode 2.7: Welcome! Happy Faces in Hawai'i

(For Attentive Listening)

Specific Use: Ages 3 to 6

Materials:

- "E Komo Mai," The Barefoot Natives, iTunes, chart of emotion faces pictured in Figure 2.5

Procedure:

1. "Please listen to my song and tell me how this music makes you feel."
2. Play track.
3. Discuss answers (happy, excited, answers will vary).
4. "Please look at my poster full of all kinds of faces. I will point to one and you tell me what feeling goes with that face."
5. Point to each face: happy, sad, angry, surprised, neutral. Field answers.
6. "Listen to my song again, and I will call on a music friend to point to the face that shows how this music makes you feel."
7. Play track.
8. Invite children individually to point to chart.
9. "You heard the words *e komo mai* in this music. This means, 'welcome!' Do you think a song that says welcome is a happy song or a sad song? What does it mean to welcome someone?"
10. Discuss answers.
11. Extend the use of this upbeat piece of music for free movement with scarves or ribbons.

Figure 2.5 Facial expression props for "E Komo Mai"

Challenges of Attentive Listening in the Early Childhood Teaching Setting

The early childhood music teaching setting presents unique challenges. Even matters as simple as the logistical manifestations of where and how music instruction can take place are complicated, though resolvable. One might posit that early childhood music instruction happens first in utero, with unborn children awash in the sonic environment of their mothers. This musical engagement continues in the home with lullabies and silly songs and games facilitated by mothers, fathers, and other caregivers in informal capacities. The childcare or daycare center may present opportunities for adults to engage young children with music. Teachers and caregivers in this setting frequently present children with music for listening, but perhaps not overtly inviting careful listening for musical constructs. More formal music classes facilitated by music professionals most certainly occur in this setting, engaging children from infancy through pre-Kindergarten in a variety of music encounters that might include listening.

It is becoming more common to see pre-Kindergarten programs cropping up in K–5 elementary school buildings, whereby young children can have their first taste of formal schooling under the roofs of real schools. These arrangements add a new dynamic to where and how early childhood music is being facilitated, and decisions must be made whether responsibilities for teaching music will be given to a certified music specialist teacher or early childhood teacher. While informal approaches are best with little ones, large class sizes and the demands of an elementary school schedule may necessitate a bit more formality.

All skilled teachers know and understand the importance of knowing their learners, knowing their developmental characteristics, knowing what they can handle in terms of musical achievement, knowing their preferences, knowing the needs and attributes of individuals and groups. Skilled teachers know that young children are not meant to be stationary by any means. They can be unpredictable—working with them might give rise to situations that must be attended to immediately (i.e., diaper changes, difficulty with transitions). Young children are thoughtful and intelligent in their listening, but this does not mean they can do so for a long span of time. They need variety in their musical encounters; they need their musical activities to flow with forward momentum.

The time and focus required for Attentive Listening can be a challenge in the early childhood realm. It can be hard to quiet the mind and body of a little one. The teacher might consider the use of focus objects like a puppet, felt visuals for a felt board, or a map, photo, or other type of prop. Manipulatives like finger puppets, scarves, and ribbons can help young children focus their attention and make their listening more concrete and relevant to their life experiences and developmental needs. These materials and implements might also assist the teacher in capturing the attention of large groups of children or children who might be having music class in a room full of distractions like toys or furniture. The captivating capabilities of props and manipulatives in the early childhood setting are illustrated in the following.

The infant and toddler music class was full of bubbly energy through the morning class. They bobbed and danced, pointed and laughed, experimented with hand drums, and got tickled by a mouse puppet. The teacher moved through activities quickly, lest the clientele lose interest and wander off to the climber or dress-up play area. The teacher saved one of the children's favorite activities for last—the clown in the cup. This prop is simply a small clown puppet attached to a wooden dowel. The teacher moved the dowel up and down to make the clown shrink and disappear into the conical cup and re-emerge at the top, much to the delight of the children present. They cheered, clapped, and shrieked at the funny little clown, pressing their hands together in the sign language gesture for "more." The teacher sang a simple tune to accompany the appearance of the clown—the tune itself is not necessarily anything special, but the presence of the clown makes the activity deeply compelling. The children reached for the clown's hands and face, danced along with his funny movements, and thrust their hands out to their sides, wrestling with their sense of object permanence, wondering, "Where did he go?"

In the next episode, the otherworldly sounds of the *sitar* may invite less structured movement on behalf of young children. Ravi Shankar has long been known as a master of the Indian instrument, the *sitar*, popularizing the modes and ethereal sounds of this traditional instrument. His work has filtered into Western popular music, as well, demonstrating a longevity and adaptability in the life of the *sitar*. Episode 2.8 asks children to characterize these potentially unfamiliar sitar sounds using descriptive words and artistic imagery. Originating in the soundscapes of Hindu temples, Indian classical music is an aurally transmitted form of music. This form of music is improvisatory and uses *ragas* as a melodic foundation. *Ragas* may reflect various moods or seasons or aspects of the natural cycles of life.

This episode invites teachers and young children to connect not only to the realm of Indian classical music, but also to the world of visual art as well. Young children regularly engage with crayons, markers, paints, and other art tools and even very vocally advertise their most favorite color. "Kafi-holi" sets the stage for children making connections among art forms, understanding and communicating the ways that artistic terms in the visual arts and music may overlap.

Episode 2.8: A Festival of Colors: The Colorful Tones of the *Sitar*

(For Attentive Listening)

Specific Use: Ages 5 to 6

Materials:

- "Kafi-holi (Spring Festival of Colors)," Ravi Shankar, iTunes, ribbons for movement, photograph of *sitar*

Procedure:

1. "Please listen to my piece of music and tell me one word that this music makes you think of."
2. Play track.
3. Discuss answers (will vary).
4. "You are hearing an instrument called a *sitar* [show photo], and the word that it makes me think of is 'colorful,' like a paint brush blending all sorts of beautiful colors on a canvas. Listen again and tell me what color this music makes you think of."
5. Play track.
6. Discuss answers (will vary).
7. "Listen again and hold up your pointer finger and 'paint' the sound of the *sitar* as you hear it."
8. Play track.
9. Respond to "paintings."
10. Extend the activity by inviting students to show the contours and bends of what they hear with a flowing scarf or ribbon.

The following lesson in Episode 2.9 challenges young children to think more broadly about what a musical instrument might be—they are not all external implements, but, rather, can be found inside the human body! Young children explore and experiment with their voices in all kinds of interesting ways yet might need the reminder that they carry a musical instrument with them at all times. This episode invites children into the rich sonic world of the African American spiritual. A type of music associated with the time of slavery in the American South, spirituals came to existence in the informal worship gatherings of slaves (frequently called camp meetings, as mentioned in this lesson recording). Many spirituals even contained messages to those looking to escape to freedom. For example, "the drinking gourd" referred to a star pattern to follow in the sky, "the Jordan river" frequently symbolized bodies of water to cross, and various Biblical characters, such as Moses, depicted helpers along the way. "Walk Together Children" remains among popular spirituals to this day, reminding the listener of the necessity of unity in troubled times and hope for what lies ahead.

Teachers may wish to set the stage for this episode, engaging young children in the myriad spirituals, songs, and games that are almost ubiquitous in the early childhood musical realm. "This Little Light of Mine" or "Amazing Grace" might ring familiar to little ones and could be avenues to gently bring them into the sound world of the spiritual. This episode works for young children on the literal level of exploring different ways to move and the more abstract level of considering the meaning of unity and how to achieve it.

Episode 2.9: Walk Together Children: Celebrating Unity With African American Spirituals

(For Attentive Listening)

Specific Use: Ages 4 to 6

Materials:

- "Walk Together Children," American Spiritual Ensemble, iTunes

Procedure:

1. "Please listen to my piece of music and tell me what instrument you hear."
2. Play track.
3. Discuss answers (voices).
4. "Listen again and tell me how the singers are telling us to move."
5. Play track.
6. Discuss answers (walk).
7. "The singers are telling us to walk together. This is a special kind of song called an African American spiritual, and one of the jobs of this kind of song is to help people feel close to each other. Listen again and pretend your hands are your feet! 'Walk' the beat on your lap."
8. Play track.
9. Assess children's beat keeping.

10. "Music friends, do you think this is really a song about walking or maybe something else? Is it a reminder to do something important?"
11. Play track.
12. Discuss answers (a call to unity).
13. "Everyone up on your feet! The song says 'walk together,' so it is very important we all keep the beat in our feet together at the same time."
14. Play track, walk about the space demonstrating the beat in the feet.
15. Extend the activity by inviting students to offer other locomotor movements to apply to this song, i.e., tiptoe together children, stomp together children, gallop together children, etc.

Teacher Feature: Dr. Anthony Leach

Dr. Anthony Leach

Dr. Anthony Leach is among the preeminent choral musicians and choral music educators in contemporary North America. A faculty member and culture-bearer at Penn State University in the U.S., Dr. Leach has brought African and African American choral music traditions not just to his university campus, but also into the consciousness of music educators on an international scale. Dr. Leach is the founder and conductor of Essence of Joy, a choral ensemble that performs musics of the African and African American traditions in the contextually and culturally appropriate ways in which they must be learned and shared. The piece featured in Episode 3.9, "Walk Together Children," is among Essence of Joy's signature processionals and is ripe with historical significance. While Dr. Leach works primarily with collegiate and adult musicians, the scope of his cultural and pedagogical expertise reaches well into the early childhood years, as evidenced in the following featured interview. Although he has described himself as a "reluctant multiculturalist," Dr. Leach's unique training and viewpoints are very helpful to teachers hoping to incorporate music of these traditions in appropriate ways.

Q: Would you please speak to your experience as a culture-bearer in the African and African American musical traditions?
A: My formal training, of course, is not in multicultural music. My informal, formal training is all immersed in African and African American choral music and musical idioms. If I had known when I was a teenager what I started to put together in my early 40s, when I came back [to Penn State] and was working on my PhD, I would have paid even more careful attention to some of the musical and life lessons that I was learning from mentors in African American music. Specifically, my professional development has been dual in that one of my mentors when I was 17, a director of music education at the First Baptist Church where I was serving as pianist for the Gospel choir, said to me,

> Leach, you gonna be ok. But let me tell you something. You're going to have to know our music and be able to do it better than anybody else but you're also going to have to know their music and be able be able to do it better than anybody else so that you will be credible.

When she shared that with me, it just rolled right off, but I was paying attention and I never forgot. Of course, as my professional journey as has morphed over the last 40 plus years, she's right.

In 2005, I took Essence [of Joy] to South Africa along with singers from my church and other guests and whatnot. Now we finally start to bridge this experience that with real encounters with people where the music is happening in real time. And we were blessed to be in a variety of schools, some churches and colleges and universities in South Africa with diverse peoples. That was great for me, it was great for the choir, but it also confirmed what I had already known and observed and read about and seen. All of a sudden now we had context and that's the real deal. I keep coming back to the fact with teachers and people that are preparing themselves to teach, if you really want to be conversational with any aspect of this music, you better be where this music is happening in real time.

Q: What advice to you have for teachers looking to bring musics of the African and African American traditions into the realm of music education?
A: I have a hierarchy. The first anchor is to sing beautifully, to sing effortlessly, to sing knowingly, meaning if there is a story behind the music, then we need to know the story. Even if we are encouraged to bring our own story, that's fine. The second one is

to move effortlessly, and the third is to clap with purpose. So, sing, move, clap. Some people get stuck as they try to go from level 1 to level 2 because once they start to sing and you ask them to move a little bit, they either get paralyzed or they've never given themselves permission to move. And then once you add clapping on top of that—oh my god! If teachers would follow that series, they will find that students or participants in these kinds of encounters will often show you very quickly what they know how to do and what they will not do without a lot of coaching and practice.

At this early childhood level, since children are trying to figure out that relationship between speech and song, we need to be aware that things that they know, what they are gleaning as they're imitating their siblings or their parents or what they see on tv or however their senses are being stimulated. What I learned a hundred years ago is that I told parents in my church choir, bring your kids. If the kids are out of control, then we'll have to deal, but bring your kids. If you can bring your kids, I've got you, but also the kids are going to learn this music just because they are hearing it. I remember in my early years at New Bethel we were doing the Hallelujah Chorus and who do you think knew their parts in the Hallelujah Chorus before the adults trusted themselves? The kids knew it and could sing every part—every part! So that's one of the many wonderful things about the African American church is this thing we call the intergenerational choir. We've always had moms and grandmommy and the kids in the choir. That's how kids come up in many communities. Everybody comes up singing, and we're not going to discuss whether you're going to church or not, you better get your butt ready, you better get dressed and ready to go and get out that door. And it happened.

Q: Can you please share your perspectives on the spiritual "Walk Together Children" in order to help teachers better understand the culture and context of this piece?
A: During the period of slavery, especially when you think about the Underground Railroad, the references to walk together of course refer to people leaving one thing in the south and making their way north. Whether it was Harriet Tubman or any number of people that were bringing people forward on the underground railroad, we look at the verses of the spiritual walk and we're not going to do a lot of walking by day. The catch line is "gonna walk and never tire," and then the next verse is "sing together children." When you think about the early church in the Black community until the slaves were allowed to gather and they sang when they gathered, sometimes that singing was outside, sometimes it was in an inside structure. Singing has been that one retention from African cultures that keeps us anchored in cultural tradition. The next verse is "pray together children." When we could not speak because we were not allowed to speak, when we knew that if we did speak either out of turn or when we were invited to speak then we might lose our life or lose a limb or our family might be separated, we could always pray. [Whether] that prayer was to God and whether one prayed verbally or one moaned or one chanted or one just thought it, that spiritual connection through prayer is what got a whole lot of people through.

The next verse is "shout together children." Well, when we think of shouting the first reference of course is to the ring shout which goes to South Carolina and Georgia, the Gullah people, the slaves off the coast. Then that same shout shows up in all of the Caribbean Islands and also in Cuba and also in South America. The shout is a circular dance, and it starts with one tempo, it gets faster and faster and faster and people get themselves caught up in the frenzy and the deal is who passes out first? The real deal as far as the tradition is concerned is you are not supposed to take your heel of your shoe off the floor, because if you take your heel off the floor then you are doing secular dancing, you're not doing church dancing, ok?

Awakening to the Possibilities

Attentive Listening launches teachers and children into the process of World Music Pedagogy. These focused listening sessions may feature musics from any and every corner of the globe, providing an effective path to both developing skill in the act of listening and getting to know the sounds and ways of cultural others. Young children are by no means "blank slates," as they do possess an openness to people and sounds and a deep-seated curiosity to explore the sonic possibilities of the world around them. While they are being awakened to many cognitive and social aspects of life in these early years, teachers would do well to meaningfully incorporate Attentive Listening to bring about cultural awakenings, as well.

Listening Episodes—Learning Pathways

"Anoai," Jacob Feuerring with Tom Hiona, Smithsonian Folkways, *hula kahiko* featuring *'uli 'uli* gourd rattles www.folkways.si.edu/hawaiian-dancers-male-singer/anoai-hula-uliuli/hawaii/music/track/smithsonian

"Moli Hua," Crystal Children's Choir & Karl Chang, iTunes, choral arrangement of traditional Chinese melody https://itunes.apple.com/WebObjects/MZStore.woa/wa/viewCollaboration?cc=us&ids=431607970-431607973

"Tera Xylophone," Music from the Villages of Northeastern Nigeria, Smithsonian Folkways, traditional xylophones of West Africa www.folkways.si.edu/music-of-the-tera-people-tera-xylophone-music/world/music/track/smithsonian

Listening Episodes

"Con Voi," Vietnamese National Song and Dance Ensemble, Smithsonian Folkways, choral/orchestral arrangement of traditional melody about elephants www.folkways.si.edu/vietnamese-national-song-and-dance-ensemble/con-voi-the-elephant/world/music/track/smithsonian

"E Komo Mai," The Barefoot Natives, iTunes, contemporary Hawaiian recording group https://itunes.apple.com/us/album/e-komo-mai/id649285502?i=649285804

"El Jilguerillo," Nati Cano's Mariachi Los Camperos, Smithsonian Folkways, famous mariachi leader and ensemble performing a love song www.folkways.si.edu/nati-canos-mariachi-los-camperos/el-jilguerillo/latin-world/music/track/smithsonian

"Kafi-holi (Spring Festival of Colors)," Ravi Shankar, iTunes, performance of world-renowned master of the *sitar* https://itunes.apple.com/us/album/kafi-holi-spring-festival-of-colors/id693524163?i=693524541

"Taiko Drumming," Taiko Drums: Music of Japan, iTunes, sampling of the percussive timbres of the *taiko* ensemble https://itunes.apple.com/us/artist/taiko-drums-music-of-japan/id291072551

"Walk Together Children," American Spiritual Ensemble, iTunes, vocal arrangement of an African American spiritual https://itunes.apple.com/us/artist/american-spiritual-ensemble/id685760744

3

Participatory Musicking

The quiet and still music classroom is empty but for Mrs. Pfeifer making her careful preparations. The guitar is tuned and set in its stand. The carpet squares are laid out neatly in rows of five. The egg shakers stand at the ready. The felt board and storybook are close at hand. Audio speakers are switched on, and the Bluetooth connection to the iPod is checked. Even a small blue ink pad and stamper are poised to be pressed into action at the end of class. The quiet does not last for long—Kindergarten is coming!

Mrs. Pfeifer greets the Kindergarten music friends at the door and directs them to their carpet squares, a routine quite familiar in this, the sixth month of the school year. Not one child chooses to walk plainly to his or her seat. Rather, they hop and bop and wiggle their way to the musical fun that lies ahead.

As they take their seats, the teacher sings, "Criss-cross applesauce, hands in your lap," a musical signal to make her behavior expectations known. Egg shakers are distributed swiftly for the hello song, with all chanting, "You get what you get and you don't get upset!" to indicate that whatever color instrument a child may receive is just fine. A few squeals of delight erupt as favorite colors are received as well as a few groans of defeat with the unwanted hues. The hello song begins with all children singing and shaking egg shakers while the teacher accompanies on the guitar. Students are invited to shake in silly ways like way up high and by their bellybuttons, but also in musically expressive ways like piano, forte, and staccato. Tiny hands reach into the air, waiting to be called on to select a way for the whole class to shake (frequently far more creative than anything the teacher could concoct herself). Their shaker skills are put to the test as they shake along with the 'uli 'uli Hawaiian gourd rattle pattern in their piece for careful listening, the hula mele "Anoai."

A brief vocal warm-up commences with a loveable snowy owl puppet, Wise Old Owl. Wise Old Owl only understands "owl language" and therefore must be greeted with light and lilting "whoooo" sounds. The class continues with a storybook made musical with a repeating tonal ostinato, a solo singing game, and a snowman movement activity where children move the melting of a snowman in various weather situations as a means to explore tempo.

For their excellent behavior, the Kindergartners are rewarded with one of their favorite silly tunes, a movement song about bubblegum and its tendency to get stuck everywhere! A goodbye song closes the children's music time. Frowns appear and groans are emitted to express sadness at the culmination of the music class, but these are soon erased by receiving stamps on their hands, a token to show to friends and family that they had music class that day. To watch these Kindergarteners in their music class is to view constant motion. Wiggles, sways, nods, arm flaps, twists, turns, stomps, shakes—they are perpetually moving, responding to the music, participating in the ways that come so very naturally to them!

Participatory Musicking

Quite simply, music is for doing! When young children hear music, whether recorded or live, their first instinct is to get involved! They may be at home, school, or out shopping or dining—their uninhibited natures shine through with their committed responses to what they hear. Dancing, singing, and playing with music come naturally to children, and teachers and caregivers can most certainly explore and develop this innate compulsion. While Chapter 2 introduces teachers and young children to the ways of Attentive Listening, Engaged Listening and Enactive Listening continue the World Music Pedagogy process with more active components. Both Engaged Listening and Enactive Listening insist on the participation of the listener in making music, in part or fully. It may be a challenge for some to move beyond listening in a consuming kind of way, but listening can truly be a gateway into getting involved, being hands-on with music in exciting ways. Music is social, brings people together, and, therefore, requires active participation. Or, as Christopher Small (1998) stated, "music is not a thing at all but an activity, something that people do" (p. 2). Small posited the term "musicking" to encompass the social, relational aspects of the doing of music, how meaning is made through bringing this art form to life.

Ethnomusicologist Thomas Turino (2008) additionally expounded upon the concept of music as something for communal doing by describing the difference between participatory and presentational music making. In the participatory framework, all individuals are invited to make music together, regardless of skill level. No one person stands out as the leader or artist; rather, all contribute what they can to the musical whole. Performances may be judged not by the quality of the music made, but by the extent to which the persons performing came together as a community. Turino contrasts this way of musicking with presentational music, which draws a distinction between those who are performing and those who are listening, as in a typical concert situation in a Western-style concert hall. Both participatory and presentational forms of musicking are found the world over, each having its own form, function, and traditions.

Turino's description of participatory music lends itself quite well to the style and preferences of early childhood music learners. Young children are very busy creatures, always with something to do, to explore, to try. They may struggle with sitting and listening to music quietly, either live or mediated, as their natural compulsion is to get up and move. In this sense, participatory musicking is perfectly congruent with the developmental needs of the early childhood world.

These participatory musicking encounters may involve improvisatory effort, allowing the children the space and freedom to experiment and try new things. Most importantly, though, these participatory opportunities provide young children with doorways to relate to other people, places, sounds, sights, values, and traditions. While facilitating these encounters with young children is not without its challenges, broadening the perspectives of little ones, inviting them into musical participation with others in the world, is well worth it.

Participating Through Engaged Listening

Listening to music of the world's cultures is not only a satisfying endeavor as an aural experience, but becomes all the richer when participatory elements are added into the mix. As addressed in Chapter 2, Attentive Listening involves the listener in careful consideration of musical constructs, laying the foundation for more active participation. Engaged Listening is the next phase of the World Music Pedagogy process, one that invites the listener to move beyond the presentational music experience into more active participation (Campbell, 2004). In this style of participatory musicking, the listeners are tasked with responding to what they hear in musical ways that might include singing, free movement, choreographed movement, or instrument play. This method of listening appeals to the musical natures of young children who seem to get involved with the music they hear without needing an invitation to do so.

Engaged Listening in the early childhood realm might take on a wide variety of child-friendly forms, the first and foremost of which is movement. Capitalizing on young children's desire to move and express is a compelling way to capture their attention and facilitate music learning. Children might be immersed in Engaged Listening experiences that intersect with their developmental needs, such as exploring large motor skills through locomotor and nonlocomotor movements, both in choreographed and free movement scenarios. Fine motor movement comes into play as well, as children might be invited to play a hand percussion instrument such as rhythm sticks or jingle bells or to perform a steady beat with a two-finger tap on their laps. Props and manipulatives might also play a role in the participatory aspect of Engaged Listening and might include ribbons, scarves, puppets, paper plates, bean bags, flashlights, or parachutes. Dances of varying types, in circles or with partners, might also serve as a way to draw young children into the world of Engaged Listening.

The hula movement tradition of Hawai'i ties into children's preference for movement. Building on the Attentive Listening episode in Chapter 2, the continuation of this Learning Pathway in Episode 3.1 calls upon children to get into the groove of the *'uli 'uli* using body percussion.

Episode 3.1: Lehua Blossoms in the Rain: Hawaiian Musical Storytelling (Learning Pathway #1)

(For Engaged Listening)

Specific Use: Ages 3 to 6

Materials:

- "Anoai," Jacob Feuerring with Tom Hiona, Smithsonian Folkways, photograph of lehua blossom, set of *'uli 'uli* or photograph, egg shakers

Procedure:

1. "Listen and try to show the rhythm of the *'uli 'uli* somewhere in your body, like your hands, feet, or shoulders.
2. Play track.
3. "This is a very special kind of music called a hula mele. It is a kind of music that tells a story. The story in this piece is about the rain drops gently falling on a lehua flower."
4. Show photograph of lehua blossom.
5. "Let's try to listen again to the rhythm of the *'uli 'uli* and put that rhythm into body percussion like this: pat pat-pat."

6. Play track.
7. Perform body percussion movements along with track.
8. "Let's listen and put the *'uli 'uli* rhythm in our hands like this: clap clap-clap."
9. Play track.
10. Perform body percussion movements along with track.
11. "Let's try putting the *'uli 'uli* pattern in our feet like this: stomp stomp-stomp."
12. Play track.
13. Perform body percussion movements along with track.
14. "This time you may put the *'uli 'uli* pattern wherever you like! Maybe you will tap your head or snap your fingers or rub your tummy! You get to choose!"
15. Play track.
16. Perform body percussion movements along with track.

Consider the Engaged Listening in Episode 3.2 and how Eurhythmic movement, that is, using the body to show characteristics of the music, might be used to reflect the programmatic element of the jasmine flower and its daily cycle of blooming and withdrawing. Through the Attentive Listening episode outlined in Chapter 2, children are primed and sensitized to the lilting of the melody, and they are readied to move into Engaged Listening through an opportunity to embody the gentle flower's mood. They are familiar with the piece, they've wondered with the teacher about the characteristics of a flower's petals and how they might be captured in music, and now they are invited to become the flower themselves. Figure 3.2 shows young children folding and unfurling their scarves to "Moli Hua."

Episode 3.2: The Gentle Jasmine: A Chinese Melody (Learning Pathway #2)

(For Engaged Listening)

Specific Use: Ages 3 to 6

Materials:

- "Moli Hua," Crystal Children's Choir & Karl Chang, iTunes, photograph of jasmine flower/vine, sun and moon visuals pictured in Figure 3.1, scarves/ribbons for dancing

Procedure:

1. "We listened to a piece of music from China about a special thing we would see in nature. Can you remember what it is?"
2. Discuss answers (flower).
3. "This piece is about a very special kind of flower called a jasmine. It does something very interesting. The petals of the flower open at nighttime and close up in the daytime. Let's listen to the voices and the *erhu* try to move like the jasmine flower does."
4. Help children find their own standing spaces in the room. Invite them to move how they think a blooming flower would look at night. Invited them to move how the petals would close during the day.

Figure 3.1 Sun and moon puppets for "Moli Hua" movement activity

5. "Let's try your jasmine flower motions with the music. When you see me hold up the sun that means it is daytime and your petals will close up. When you see me hold up the moon that means it is nighttime and your petals will open up."
6. Play track. Display sun and moon, children move accordingly.

Figure 3.2 Children in the midst of Engaged Listening to "Moli Hua"

Consider, also, the following lesson sequence that picks up where the Attentive Listening episode left off. In Episode 3.3, children are invited to take a rudimentary step towards performing West African polyrhythms with two simple rhythmic patterns for body percussion performance.

Episode 3.3: X Marks the Spot: Xylophones of West Africa (Learning Pathway #3)

(For Engaged Listening)

Specific Use: Ages 5 to 7

Materials:

- "Tera Xylophone," Music from the Villages of Northeastern Nigeria, Smithsonian Folkways, Boomwhackers (Ab, Db, Eb), tone bells (Db, Eb, F, Ab, Bb), photograph of West African xylophone

Procedure:

1. "Listen to my xylophone music from West Africa again and tell me if you hear lots of different rhythms or just a steady beat. Pat the beat on your lap to help you figure out the answer."
2. Play track.
3. Discuss answers (lots of different rhythms).
4. "Let's try to make some different rhythms in our class. Half of you will pat a steady beat on your lap and half of you will do a two-finger tap to one of the xylophone rhythms (ti-ti ti-ti ta rest)."

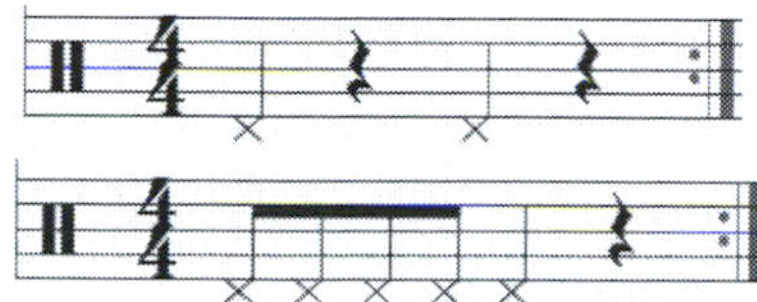

5. Divide class in half and assign task.
6. Play track.
7. Model steady beat for one group.
8. Model rhythm pattern for the other group.
9. Repeat, trading roles.

Young children love to be involved, to be engaged, to try new things, to feel the empowerment that comes with musical independence. They also love to explore the boundaries of what their voices and bodies can do. Episode 3.4 brings the loveable and long-lasting American folk music sensibilities of Pete Seeger into the aural realm of young children. The son of musicologist and composer Charles Seeger, Pete Seeger has long been known for his banjo-infused American folk music repertoire coupled with his social activist agenda. Having been blacklisted during the McCarthy era in the early 1950s due to his political affiliations, Pete Seeger became more involved in performing music for children, resulting in recordings like the one featured here. In this lesson, young children are engaged through the vocal exploration of farm animal sounds. While this may seem like a questionable pedagogical objective, one should remember that the singing voice is an emergent skill during early childhood and that vocal exploration, from speech to song and including sounds of machinery, animals, and nature, is key in its development. Teachers may choose to add the sign language for each of these animals to add a kinesthetic component. The folk song "Bought Me a Cat" and the musical stylings of Pete Seeger draw young children into the themes and sounds of the days of rural America, where a hard day's work on the farm meant caring for animals and crops. A window into the past, this episode bridges the gap between the agrarian roots of America and the beloved animal friends of today.

Episode 3.4: Farm Fun in the U.S.

(For Engaged Listening)

Specific Use: Ages 1 to 6

Materials:

- "Bought Me a Cat," Pete Seeger, iTunes, animal puppets or pictures (optional)

Procedure:

1. "Please listen to my song and tell me what the cat said?."
2. Play first verse of track.
3. Discuss answers (fiddle-i-dee).
4. "Is fiddle-i-dee what cats really say? Let's try to make a real cat sound!"
5. All meow as a vocal exploration exercise.
6. "Let's listen to my song again and make the animal sounds we hear."
7. Play track. Make sounds of each animal.
8. To extend this activity, especially with very young children, incorporate the sign language for each animal in the song.

Musical Transmission and Engagement

Consider the absurdity of the following scenario. An infant, in order to learn the sounds and ways of speaking his native language, is taken to a weekly baby language class. He sits in a high chair desk along with several other babies, faces the chalkboard, and learns the particulars of the language of his culture of origin. His caregiver picks him up from class and notices his homework planner with the assignment to practice saying the word "mama." If he masters this word by the next class, he will receive a sticker on his progress chart.

While this is a ridiculous notion to contemplate, hopefully it draws attention to the fact that the initial days and years of learning a language are not a formal affair, but, rather, an endeavor that takes place over time, informally, observing and absorbing the sounds and meanings of words from family members and caregivers. In much of the world, it is this way with music. Children in their early years do not attend a formal music class to learn the nuts and bolts of the theoretical array of melodic sequences, chord progressions, and part writing. They watch, hear, and do the music along with their families, friends, and community members. Immersion is the preferred mode of learning music in many cultures, one that invites full participation from the very beginning.

Children may further their exploration of the music and movement traditions of Hawai'i through engaging with the hula mele "E Pele Pele Pele" in Episode 3.5. An important character in Hawaiian mythology, Pele is the often-temperamental volcano goddess, whose imperious ways are woven into many stories and legends. Among these legends is Pele's pan–Pacific Ocean journey to find a home, finally settling in Hawai'i—this mele retells this tale.

Episode 3.5: Dramatic Dance: The Hula of Hawai'i

(For Engaged Listening)

Specific Use: Ages 5 to 6

Materials:

- "E Pele Pele Pele," Jacob Feuerring and Tom Hiona, Smithsonian Folkways, small hand drums (6 inch recommended), Pele Tapping Page (Figure 3.3)

Procedure:

1. "Please listen to my piece of music and tell me what instruments you hear."
2. Play track.
3. Discuss answers (drum and voice)
4. Play brief excerpt of track and check answers.
5. "Can you listen again and pretend play the drum beat on your lap?"
6. Play track.
7. Respond to beat keeping.
8. "Was the drum beat always the same or did it change?"

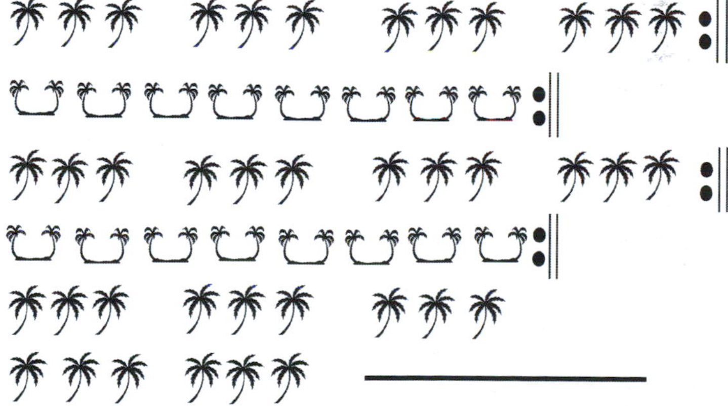

Figure 3.3 Rhythmic tapping page for "E Pele Pele Pele"

9. Play track to assess.
10. Discuss answers (varied between micro/macro beats)
11. "This music is for dancing hula, which is a traditional Hawaiian dance that is used to tell stories. This piece tells of the Volcano goddess, Pele, who was looking for a home in the Pacific Ocean. She finally found one in Hawai'i."
12. Distribute hand drums to students. Play micro/macro beats on the drum, alternating hands.

13. Play track.
14. Assess beat keeping and hand drum technique.
15. Extend this activity into a discussion of form with the Pele Tapping Page. Tap a finger on the top of each palm tree in order to keep track of the beats.

It is interesting to consider not only the various cultures of the world and their preferred modes of musical transmission, but also the concept of children as constructors of their own musical culture. Children naturally engage with music in playful ways, combining song, speech, and movement in endless combinations. No matter their cultural heritage, they teach each other and learn from each other through imitation, observation, and immersion in the world of musical play, passing on repertoire that lives for generations and is transmitted all over the globe. Handclapping games, jump rope chants, circle games, song parodies, and more capture the imaginations and musical natures of children all over the world. The aural-oral nature of the transmission of these playful repertoires allows children to make them their own, putting their own personal musical, stylistic stamps on the sometimes ubiquitous tunes and chants of childhood. If immersion, observation, absorption, and participation are preferred modes of being musical when children have the ability to choose their own way of musicking, and these are the preferred modes of many of the world's cultures, it makes sense to bring this style of musical transmission into the lives of young children.

Engaged Listening, capitalizing upon the immersive way of teaching and learning music in many cultures, may stand in contrast to the preference of other cultures to learn music "by eye" rather than "by ear." Many systems of musical notation exist for musicians to document the sounds they wish to create or reproduce. Ideally, a balance may be struck between the two, providing the freedom to explore the world's musical cultures through a variety of means.

Children's natural movement tendencies lend themselves well to the following Engaged Listening activity in which they are asked to move according to the form of the piece using a parachute. With all children grasping onto the parachute, this prop creates an opportunity for early childhood music learners to develop ensemble skills. Additionally, the parachute is bright and immediately appealing to little ones for music play. However, the skilled teacher must set some appropriate ground rules for its use, such as no stepping on top of the parachute or running under the parachute. Belgian composer Pierre Leemans was known during the 20th century for a variety of styles of composition, but most notably his marches. The "March of the Belgian Paratroopers" was written during the World War II era in response to the formation of a Belgian parachute corps. The "March of the Belgian Paratroopers" in Episode 3.6 presents a fun play on words while allowing children the ability to keep pace with the graceful ease of a European march. While little ones are too young to discuss in detail the intricacies of European wartime tactics in the earlier half of the 20th century, they most certainly can relate to the steady beat of a march, understanding that music can be a way to help people stay together—both in moving rhythmically from place to place as well as in unified spirit.

Episode 3.6: Parachuting to Belgium!

(For Engaged Listening)

Specific Use: Ages 3 to 7

Materials:

- "March of the Belgian Paratroopers," Eastern Wind Symphony, iTunes, small parachute with handles

Procedure:

1. "Listen to my piece of music and tell me how you could move your feet to this music"
2. Play track.
3. Discuss answers.
4. "This is a kind of music called a march. Stand up in your spot and march to the beat!"
5. Play track.
6. "This march is called the 'March of the Belgian Paratroopers.' Paratroopers use big parachutes to float on the air. Let's try a parachute dance to go with this special march."
7. Assemble children around the perimeter of the parachute.
8. Play track and perform the dance as described here.

Dance Maneuvers and Form

Introduction—Get Ready!

A: March into center of parachute for 4 beats, out for 4 Repeat

B: Rotate Counterclockwise

A: In for 4, out for 4 Repeat

C: Float Up and Down 4x (raise up over head and back down)

A: In for 4, out for 4 Repeat

D: Gentle Fluff (gently move the parachute to make small waves)

E: Washing Machine (move parachute to right and then left, alternating sides)

A: In for 4, out for 4 Repeat

B: Rotate Counterclockwise

A: In for 4, out for 4 Repeat

Coda: Gentle Fluff and Drop

Young children will love to get involved with the sassy *samba* beats of Brazil in this next episode. Samba is a dance commonly found in Brazil, but it most certainly has ties to the African diaspora. Throughout the African slave trade years, individuals were relocated, bringing their musical expressions along with them. The marriage of African musical elements with Brazilian music and dance has created an exciting genre of music and dance that continues to evolve, showcasing the unique expressive qualities of this South American nation. Episode 3.7 will undoubtedly get children moving and feeling the "quick-quick slow" pattern of the samba steps, first presented as body percussion. As children get the hang of it, they might be ready to get up and try some samba steps!

Episode 3.7: Samba Style

(For Engaged Listening)

Specific Use: Ages 3 to 7

Materials:

- "Samba," Dances of the World's Peoples Volume III, Smithsonian Folkways

Procedure:

1. "Music friends, I am going to play a piece of music for you, and I want you listen and guess what this kind of music would be used for."
2. Play track.
3. Field answers.
4. "If you were thinking that this music is for dancing you would be correct! Listen again and tell me where you think this dance music comes from."
5. Play track.
6. Field answers.
7. "Brazil is the name of the country where this dance music, called samba, comes from. It is very special, though, because different kinds of music from

all over the world all came together to make samba what it is. There are samba steps for our feet, but let's try them with our hands first. It goes like this: quick-quick slow, quick-quick slow. Show me that pattern with a two-finger tap. Pay close attention because the pattern happens very quickly."

8. Practice pattern.
9. "Let's try it with the music!"
10. Play track. Tap the quick-quick slow pattern.
11. Extend the episode by inviting children to put the quick-quick slow pattern into their feet.

Participating Through Enactive Listening

As stated previously, music is for doing, and that is no different for young children. With the exploration of world music beginning with Attentive Listening, taking note of musical elements, moving to Engaged Listening, which invites participation of some types, the process next moves to Enactive Listening, presenting children with the opportunity to launch performances of the world music selections rooted in their careful listening. Enactive Listening extends the seeds planted in Engaged Listening, with young children producing musical sounds both with the recordings and on their own. As such, repeated listening encounters are necessary to ensure children's success, allowing them to become immersed in the sounds they hear, setting the stage to join in themselves. One should note that it is important to keep with the appropriate style of the cultures represented. However, the adept teacher of early childhood music will understand that adaptations will likely need to be made to accommodate the developmental age and stage of young children, accounting for motor skills, vocal development, and attention span.

"Anoai" returns again, this time bringing children into the realm of Enactive Listening, replacing the *'uli 'uli* body percussion pattern with child-friendly egg shakers that simulate the sounds of the Hawaiian gourd rattles. While young children may be unable to effectively chant this mele in the Hawaiian language, they can most certainly perform the rhythms of the accompanying traditional instrument in Episode 3.8.

Episode 3.8: Lehua Blossoms in the Rain: Hawaiian Musical Storytelling (Learning Pathway #1)

(For Enactive Listening)

Specific Use: Ages 3 to 6

Materials:

- "Anoai," Jacob Feuerring with Tom Hiona, Smithsonian Folkways, photograph of lehua blossom, set of *'uli 'uli* or photograph, egg shakers

Procedure:

1. "Try to remember our song about the rain gently falling on the lehua blossoms. We learned about the *'uli 'uli* that makes the sound of the rain. Listen and do your body percussion movements to the *'uli 'uli* part."
2. Play track.
3. Perform pat pat pat clap-clap body percussion movements.
4. 
5. "Does the *'uli 'uli* remind you of any other instrument you have played before?"
6. Discuss answers (shakers, maracas, etc.)
7. "Let's play our body percussion part on egg shakers so we can sound just like the *'uli 'uli*."
8. Distribute egg shakers to children.
9. Play track.
10. Play the ta ta ta ti-ti pattern on egg shakers.
11. Extend this activity by inviting children to try the basic hula vamp step of kaholo.

    Step right—touch-step right-touch
    Step left—touch-step left-touch
    Repeat

Episode 3.9 brings students from the moments of Attentive Listening for musical mood to Engaged Listening with Eurhythmic movement. This Enactive Listening encounter facilitates a singing performance of "Moli Hua" in addition to a movement performance of the programmatic elements of the piece. Repeated listening encounters will set young children up for success in learning this melody.

Episode 3.9: The Gentle Jasmine: A Chinese Melody (Learning Pathway #2)

(For Enactive Listening)

Specific Use: Ages 3 to 6

Materials:

- "Moli Hua," Crystal Children's Choir & Karl Chang, iTunes, photograph of jasmine flower/vine, sun and moon visuals, scarves/ribbons for dancing

Procedure:

1. Play track. Display sun and moon visuals to prompt children's movement.
2. "You have all done such a good job moving like the jasmine flower does during different times of day. Here is what this song means in English."
3. Read translation.
4. "You have heard this song enough times to try to sing along! If you have trouble saying the Chinese words, you may sing on the word 'loo' until you get them."
5. Play track. Sing along.
6. Help children find their own space in the room.
7. Distribute scarves or ribbons for movement.
8. Children may sing along to the melody and then move freely during the interludes.

English Translation

What a beautiful jasmine,
What a beautiful jasmine,
Fragrance and beauty fill every branch.
Fragrant and white, everyone praises it.
Let me pluck for you.
To give to others.
Jasmine, Jasmine.

Episode 3.10 presents children with yet another opportunity for participatory Enactive Listening. As they began in the way of Attentive Listening with instrument identification and Engaged Listening with body percussion work, they now enter the possibilities of Enactive Listening through the use of Boomwhackers (pictured in Figure 3.4) and tone bells, child-friendly substitutions that will allow little ones access to sound production.

Episode 3.10: X Marks the Spot: Xylophones of West Africa (Learning Pathway #3)

(For Enactive Listening)

Specific Use: Ages 5 to 7

Materials:

- "Tera Xylophone," Music from the Villages of Northeastern Nigeria, Smithsonian Folkways, Boomwhackers (Ab, Db, Eb), color-coded paper to match Boomwhackers, tone bells (Db, Eb, F, Ab, Bb), photograph of West African xylophone

Procedure:

1. "You all did a great job patting the steady beat and tapping the xylophone rhythm pattern. Instead of tapping our hands or patting our laps, let's add some instruments."
2. Divide children into steady beat group and rhythm pattern group.
3. Distribute Ab and Db Boomwhackers to steady beat group.
4. Play track.
5. Steady beat group plays their instruments.

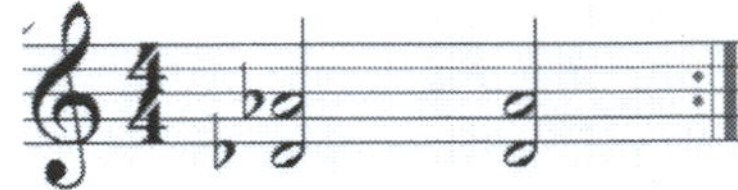

6. Distribute additional Db Boomwhackers and Eb Boomwhackers.
7. Use color-coded paper to rehearse the rhythm/tonal pattern.

8. Play track.
9. Steady beat group begins.
10. Rhythm pattern group is layered in.

Figure 3.4 Playing Boomwhackers

As some levels of instrumental or vocal performance may be beyond the scope of what is developmentally appropriate for young children in their early childhood years, teachers would do well to launch culturally authentic performances of singing games. These little gems from the world's cultures are learned by listening, as are any other musical selections, and can progress through the first dimensions of World Music Pedagogy all the way to Enactive Listening. In fact, young children require extensive listening, from Attentive, to Engaged, to Enactive levels, in order to make their way to the "performance" of these singing games at full capacity. Children across the globe engage in singing games, which further suggests that this genre of musical play might be a familiar point of entry for many. "Tyven Tyven" (Episode 3.11) is a delightful game from the northern land of Norway where children can choose (or, as the children may say, "steal") their partners, exercising their autonomy as they connect with their Norwegian friends. Participating in many listening encounters with "Tyven Tyven" allows children the opportunity to both learn to sing along and offer a turn in the game to all involved.

Episode 3.11: Thief! Thief! Finding Friends With Norwegian Folk Dance

(For Enactive Listening)

Specific Use: Ages 5 to 7

Materials:

- "Tyven Tyven" Veslemøy Fjerdingstad, iTunes

Procedure:

1. "Please stand up, listen to my song, and put the beat in your feet."
2. Play track.
3. Assess beat keeping.
4. "We are going to play a game with this song. Everyone needs a partner and to stand in a circle with their partner."
5. Assist children in finding partners, form a circle with sets of two partners holding hands, facing counterclockwise.
6. Assign one "thief" to the center of the circle. During the A Section of the song, the children move forward in the circle. When the children hear "tror jeg tra la la," the thief may tap someone on the shoulder, indicating that the thief would like to steal that person's partner. The thief takes that child's place, and the displaced partner enters the middle to become the new thief.
7. During the B Section of the song, the circle halts and the partners dance with one another as they wish.

8. Note: There are variations to this folk dance, some including fast and furious partner switches—the provided interpretation is intended to keep the game manageable and small children safe.

Song Translation

Thief, thief shall you be called
For you stole my little friend.
But I have a hope in waiting,
That I soon get one again.

The early childhood years are a wonderful time for teachers and caregivers to imagine the possibilities that their little musicians will explore in the future. They prepare young children to be rhythmically accurate, to use a healthy singing voice, to listen carefully, to connect to other art forms and cultures, to demonstrate appropriate instrument technique, and to develop ensemble skills. Perhaps many young children will go on to sing or play in group situations. In these ensemble settings young children need to know that it is not always their turn to sing or play, but they must remain focused in order to know when to enter the music. Further, they must understand that the music is being made by a whole team to which they are a contributor. Episode 3.12 offers an Enactive Listening opportunity that cultivates these ensemble skills in a child-friendly way. "Escravos de Jó" presents children with an opportunity to connect with their South American counterparts in Brazil through a choreographed passing game that is popular in various manifestations among the children there. This tune is a popular game among little ones of that region (and older ones, too!) and involves the passing of a manipulative to a steady beat. Anything will do for passing—Brazilian children have even been known to do this at the dinner table with cutlery or glasses! This episode can even serve as a follow-up to the lesson on samba.

Episode 3.12: Working as a Team With Brazilian Beats

(For Enactive Listening)

Specific Use: Ages 6 to 7

Materials:

- "Escravos de Jó," Dino Lingo, iTunes, manipulatives for passing (i.e., rocks, wooden cubes, rhythm sticks, egg shakers)

Procedure:

1. "Listen to my piece of music and tell me what you think this song might be used for."

2. Play track.
3. Discuss answers.
4. "This is a game song! It is a passing game where we work as a team."
5. Form a seated circle on the floor. Place one hand in front. Begin a "pick pass" motion to a steady beat where picking up an object is mimed in front of the body and pass is mimed letting go of the object in front of the person to the immediate right.
6. Play track while practicing the "pick pass" motion.
7. Assess students' beat keeping. If they are demonstrating a steady beat, they may try the "pick pass" with one object such as a wooden cube, rhythm stick, egg shaker, or rock.
8. Play track while passing the object.
9. To extend this activity give each child an object to pass so they are continually passing throughout the game.
10. To extend this activity further, add the following choreography:
    a. On "tira" pick the object up and hold it up and back away from the circle.
    b. On "bota" put the object back into the circle.
    c. On "deixa ficar" tap the object on the floor three times.

Song Text

Escravos de Jó jogavam Caxangá
Tira Bota, deixa ficar.
Guerreiros com guerreiros fazem zigue zigue za.
Guerreiros com guerreiros fazem zigue zigue za.

Translation

Slaves of Jó played Caxangá
Put it back, take it out, let it stay
Warriors with warriors play zig-zig-zag
Warriors with warriors play zig-zig-zag
(translated by Juliana Cantarelli Vita)

The *didjeridu* presents a compelling entry point for studying the music of the indigenous peoples of Australia. Young children are naturally drawn to learning about musical instruments and may have never heard the deep, vibrating tones of the *didjeridu*, a long, cylindrical wooden instrument used for centuries by indigenous Australians. This instrument has some commonalities with brass instruments that may be more familiar to children in that the player must buzz his lips together to produce a sound—young children would undoubtedly be delighted to give that a try! Children may be interested to learn about the circular breathing technique that *didjeridu* players must employ in order to maintain continuous sound. Episode 3.13 invites children into this centuries-old sound world of the *didjeridu*. In the listening excerpt provided, children will also hear the voice and tapping sticks. With their own rhythm sticks, children will have no problem joining in with the beat.

Episode 3.13: Down Under With the *Didjeridu*

(For Enactive Listening)

Specific Use: Ages 4 to 7

Materials:

- "Australia: Morning Star, Pigeon and Rain Songs," Musical Sources, Smithsonian Folkways, rhythm sticks

Procedure:

1. "In my piece of music, you will hear a very interesting instrument you may never have heard before. Please listen carefully and tell me one word you would use to describe this instrument."
2. Play track.
3. Field answers.
4. "This interesting instrument is called a *didjeridu* and comes from Australia. Listen again and tell me what you think this instrument is made of."
5. Play track.
6. Field answers.
7. "*Didjeridus* are made out of wood. Do you know any other instruments that are made from wood?"
8. Field answers.
9. "Listen again and tell me if you hear any other types of sounds or instruments."
10. Play track.
11. Field answers (voice and rhythm sticks).
12. "It is your turn to join in! Your job is to play your rhythm sticks along with the beat you hear in the recording."
13. Distribute rhythm sticks.
14. Play track and tap along.

Any musical genre that serves to facilitate movement and dance is sure to capture the imagination and encourage the participation of young children. Episode 3.14 whisks children away to Spain and the vigorous strums of guitars, the soulful singing, and the percussive slaps and taps of hands and feet. Flamenco is a multimodal musical expression hailing from Spain featuring instrumental performance, dance, singing, and body percussion. With roots in Andalusia, the flowing costumes and committed performances of flamenco draw in children and adults alike. This episode invites children to consider body percussion as a way of contributing to a musical entity, encouraging them to listen carefully and join in with their feet!

Episode 3.14: Flamenco Feet

(For Enactive Listening)

Specific Use: Ages 4 to 7

Materials:

- "Cuadro Flamenco," Spain: Flamenco Music of Andalusia, Smithsonian Folkways

Procedure:

1. "Please listen to my piece of music and tell me what kinds of sounds you hear."
2. Play track.
3. Field answers.
4. "While you heard a guitar, you probably heard some other sounds, too. Maybe these sounds are not traditional instruments—they might be things you have with you right now! Listen and try to figure out what you hear."
5. Play track.
6. Field answers.
7. "Music friends, this type of music is called flamenco and comes from the country of Spain. Flamenco is very exciting because it combines instruments, singing, dancing, and even body percussion. You heard lots of claps and even the sounds of shoes tapping on the floor. Let's listen again and see if you can make some flamenco tapping sounds on the floor, too!"
8. Play track.
9. Dance along.

Challenges to Engaged and Enactive Listening for Early Childhood

Teachers must never underestimate what young children can do musically and what they can do with music. They must find a balance between the demands of the participatory musicking and the developmental ages and stages of early childhood music learners. It is important for the little ones to be active, up and moving, creating and responding, but the attention spans of little ones must be carefully considered, and the episodes and lessons should be tailored and timed so to get the most out of them while they are attentive and fresh. Other adaptations for this age group might involve altering the complexity of rhythmic and tonal patterns that children are asked to perform, allowing children to participate authentically, but in ways they will be set up to be successful. Adaptations of instruments are also a consideration, contemplating how instruments might be scaled or made to fit small children's hands or the substitution of child-sized instruments (e.g., a 6-inch hand drum replacing a large frame drum). Other instrument substitutions might include Orff barred percussion instruments for West African xylophones, egg shakers for gourd rattles, rhythm sticks for guiros, and Boomwhackers for drone instruments. The child's vocal instrument must be considered as well and may involve the re-working of ranges and tessituras to accommodate the child's healthy vocal usage.

Nancy Youmans Playing Ukulele With Students

Mrs. Nancy Youmans teaches K–5 music in a public school district in a community near a large state university. She teaches 30 classes per week in addition to extracurricular choral groups. Prior to her current position, Mrs. Youmans was involved with children ages 2 through 6 in a Montessori school where she taught both music and regular classroom instruction.

World Music Pedagogy is rooted in the foundational musical act of listening. Mrs. Youmans has worked to create gateways of deep, intelligent listening for her students through the application of the practice of mindfulness. Mindfulness entails centering one's self, staying in the present moment, focusing on what is happening right now, and dealing gently with distracting thoughts. Calming one's thoughts and recognizing rogue thoughts frees the listener to notice what is happening in the music. When distractions occur in the mind, Mrs. Youmans explained that one must "recognize them with kindness and curiosity" and find a way to get back to the present musical moment. Mrs. Youmans has studied mindfulness in order to benefit her own teaching but has found it to be a powerful tool in encouraging students to "understand what it really means to listen."

Q: Could you describe your philosophy of listening to music in the early childhood setting?
A: I guess part of my philosophy is to be able to have kids to be able to understand what it truly means to listen, first of all, and to practice that. At that age, and even as they get older, everything really needs to be practiced multiple times to comprehend what we're talking about. But the way everything is right now, like right now we're listening to music [referring to background music at coffee shop]—a lot of their early experience is that music is something you are not just listening to and focusing on. It's going on in the background of your life and you're not really listening to it. I guess my philosophy is to try to get them to actually listen to the music.

Q: Could you describe your work with mindfulness and how you make use of that practice in listening lessons with young children?
A: I've done research the last year and a half or so with mindfulness in general. The main guru for that is Patricia Jennings and her *Mindfulness for Teachers* book. She was a music teacher for several years, so a lot of her philosophies and the way she talks about [mindfulness] is in a very music-based way which is helpful for me. I've taken some classes through my school district on how to be mindful myself and then also how to teach my students to be mindful. I took that and I made it more of a music listening activity. The main point is to calm your thoughts. By having your thoughts calm and not having so many thoughts running through your head, you're then able to notice things. That's the main point. Focus just means being able to notice things. Introducing it to kids through music—I give them different options for techniques for listening. I tell them what they could be listening for but I tell them they don't have to. Things they can do with their bodies that can help calm them. What to do when they do have distracting thoughts, playing through those scenarios, a thought comes through your head, "What's for lunch today?" "What am I going to do after school today?" "I wonder if I'll have any homework later?" and recognizing those [distracting thoughts] with kindness and curiosity. Those are the two big words in [this process]. So I notice, "Oh that doesn't have anything to do with the music I'm listening to." I'm going to notice it kindly and I'm going say, "Oh, that's interesting" and [the students and I] talk about different things we can do with those distracting thoughts and then try to bring [ourselves] back into the music. We talk about lots of examples but then we just try it. I give them a time. I'll say, "Ok, we're going to listen to this piece for one minute and when we get to the end of it, what did you notice? If you're comfortable sharing, what did you notice?" And then I get lots of responses about what they noticed, what they didn't notice. Some of them talk about the music specifically, about their response to the music. Some of them talk about their distractions or not being distracted. In doing those [exercises], I feel that when we come back and just listen to the music without having this formal "now we're going to mindfully listen to music" that I'm getting them to be able to more immediately actually focus on the music. I'm getting a lot of good responses. With the little ones [Kindergarten], I've added something new this year. I have little silicone spots. They're not very big, they're thin, they're colorful, and they feel cool. The kids love them. They're smooth, they can roll them up easily. I give them a choice. I say some people find them distracting when they're trying to

mindfully listen, and if you do, you can go back to sitting on them, which is what they do for the rest of the music class. Or you can put them in front of you and have that be your focus spot, because some kids don't like to close their eyes. Or you can hold them in your hand and rub them while you're listening. Sometimes people need a focus or an anchor. So then I have kids make a variety of choices. Those [silicone spots] have really helped. Even before I introduced mindfulness, just to have them playing with those while they listen to the music, I feel, has focused them without them even knowing it. They're not talking, they're just playing by themselves. I use the word "play." That's another thing they do to be able to focus. It is mindfully related without labelling it as "now we're going to try to do this." I do this with Kindergarten and first grade.

Q: When I was in your classroom last semester and I saw the Kindergartners listening with the spots, I thought it was so remarkable how many of them used those spots musically. As if to interpret the pitch or the tempo of what they were hearing. Have you noticed things like that evolving through this process?

A: Yes, I have noticed that as well. When they first get [the silicone spots], their main goal is to make shapes out of them. But then as they get comfortable with them as the weeks go on, they do that. They move it up and down, they're making it go smooth, almost like a scarf, a Dalcroze kind of a thing. I make no comment about that, no "maybe you could try . . . " I've said nothing, just let them see where it takes them. I have seen that quite a bit with them. I've thought about maybe trying to direct that a little bit but I kind of don't want to. I almost want it to be [theirs]. Then when we do go to talk about those things, that connection will be there without naming it.

Q: It's just amazing to see 25 tiny little ones in that [musical] moment. You had mentioned that you give them options for things to listen for or options for things to do with their bodies as they listen. What are some of those things?

A: I'll say to them that it helps to have a focus. In my training, in my mindfulness class, it was made very clear, don't ever tell kids to close their eyes. Don't make that a rule, because there are some people that you don't know what they're going through and it's a very scary thing to close their eyes. Which makes perfect sense. So I say to them,

> If you feel comfortable, you can close your eyes. That helps me block out distractions because this room has so many things that are exciting to look at and distract my thoughts. If you don't, that's fine, too. But, if you don't, pick a spot, maybe not up on the walls where all the crazy stuff is, maybe a spot on the floor or maybe your hands are resting in your lap. You can look down at your hands.

One little girl said, "I have flowers on my pants today, and I just picked a flower and looked at that the whole time." They come up with their own little things. But it's surprising how many of them do close their eyes and enjoy that.

I do not allow them to lie down because I want them attentive. I don't want them falling asleep. Their brains are working, they are choosing to listen to something so they sit up, hands gently resting in their laps, in a relaxed position. As to what they could listen to—I say to them,

> Here are some things that I've tried that help me stay focused. Sometimes I listen to what instruments I'm hearing. Sometimes I think about how the music

> makes me feel. And sometimes I even have a little movie playing in my head about what could be happening while the music is playing. Someone's picking flowers, someone's skiing down a hill, someone's ice skating, so you can have a little movie playing in your head and that's focusing. But if you start thinking about what you're going to do after school, then that's a distraction and you need to try to bring it back.

I've had kids tell me they had a distracting thought, but they morphed it into relating to the music, which I thought was kind of interesting! Other kids will say that they really were actually not thinking of anything. [One child said,] "I felt like I was on a big stage and I wasn't thinking of anything I was just kind of floating." And I thought, that's kind of advanced meditation right there! Through my other learning, the response is always "good to know" so that you are not making any judgement, trying not to put too much of my own labels on it. I use the phrase, "What do you notice?" and that helps a lot with listening to music. What do you notice? I always start with 1 minute—some of them, when the time is up, they are disappointed. They really seem to enjoy the "permission" to just listen to the music.

Q: I wonder if that is a commentary on how stimulated children are?
A: I think it very much is. I do see several of them, when we start, it takes them a moment [to get into the music]. The other part of it is the brain and what is actually happening. If you have too many things going on at once, you literally can't focus on something. Until you calm [yourself] you can't focus. They describe it like a snow globe that's shook up all the time. We all know what that feels like, and I talk about that with the Kindergarten kids, too. "Do you know what a snow globe is? When you shake it up, what's the snow doing?" "Oh, it's all over." "Right, well, sometimes your thoughts are like that. How do you make the snow calm down?" "Oh, we hold it still."

Q: Very sophisticated metacognition happening at 5 years old!
A: [I tell them] it's really like building up your focusing muscles.

Q: Can you speak to some world cultures that you incorporate into your listening?
A: With all the grades [early childhood years included], I do a lot of listening to multicultural music. [Some grades will do] a trip around the world where each class has a passport. It's two weeks' worth of each country. We watch videos, listen to music, and learn a piece and perform it. At the end of the second week, they have to perform [the piece of music] and answer questions based on it. I try to do things like games and play instruments from as many [cultures] as I can.

Q: Do you feel like your Kindergartners and first graders, and your past preschoolers, are receptive to hearing these sounds from around the world?
A: Definitely. They actually like that a lot. They especially like games or dances, because I think they like picturing somebody that they have never even met, that they would do that too. The little African rock game that we play, kids play this, and they say "wow!" They really like that, and I think they like listening to different sounds. They're very receptive and like learning to sing in different languages, too.

Q: If there are teachers who are interested in using mindfulness to get more world music into their students' diet, where would you recommend they start?
A: Definitely with the book *Mindfulness for Teachers* [by Patricia Jennings] because it can be applied to the music classroom. It's a two-part book—it helps you to be mindful yourself in your own teaching, attentive to how you're interpreting things, and then also it helps in teaching your students to be mindful. All the things I'm doing with listening to music, I've just kind of come up with myself, but it's not that big of a jump. I really think people could do this themselves. That book is my bible of how to do this!

Getting Hands-on with Music

Engaged Listening and Enactive Listening provide scaffolds for teachers to bring young children into more active encounters with the world's musical cultures. Moving from Attentive Listening activities into the realms of kinesthetic and musical doing sets little ones up for success in terms of developing an aural awareness of the unique characteristics of the world's musical cultures to which they are exposed. After all, musicking around the globe is not static or stationary—people are hands-on with their music, just as young children should be.

References

Campbell, P. S. (2004). *Teaching music globally*. New York, NY: Oxford University Press.

Jennings, P. A. (2015). *Mindfulness for teachers: Simple skills for peace and productivity in the classroom*. New York, NY: W.W. Norton & Company.

Small, C. (1998). *Musicking*. Middletown, CT: Wesleyan University Press.

Turino, T. (2008). *Music as social life: The politics of participation*. Chicago, IL: University of Chicago Press.

Listening Episodes—Learning Pathways

"Anoai," Jacob Feuerring with Tom Hiona, Smithsonian Folkways, *hula kahiko* featuring *'uli 'uli* gourd rattles www.folkways.si.edu/hawaiian-dancers-male-singer/anoai-hula-uliuli/hawaii/music/track/smithsonian

"Moli Hua," Crystal Children's Choir & Karl Chang, iTunes, choral arrangement of traditional Chinese melody https://itunes.apple.com/WebObjects/MZStore.woa/wa/viewCollaboration?cc=us&ids=431607970-431607973

"Tera Xylophone," Music from the Villages of Northeastern Nigeria, Smithsonian Folkways, traditional xylophones of West Africa www.folkways.si.edu/music-of-the-tera-people-tera-xylophone-music/world/music/track/smithsonian

Listening Episodes

"Bought Me a Cat," Pete Seeger, iTunes, classic American folk song sung by renowned American folk singer https://itunes.apple.com/us/album/bought-me-a-cat/id103487559?i=103487610 (up to 2:15 only)

"E Pele Pele Pele," Jacob Feuerring with Tom Hiona, Smithsonian Folkways, *hula kahiko* telling a story of Pele the Hawaiian volcano goddess www.folkways.si.edu/hawaiian-dancers-male-singer/e-pele-pele-pele-hawaiian-drama-hula/hawaii/music/track/smithsonian

"Samba," Dances of the World's Peoples Volume III, Smithsonian Folkways, music for Brazilian samba dancing https://folkways.si.edu/samba/caribbean-world/music/track/smithsonian

"Tyven Tyven," Veslemøy Fjerdingstad, iTunes, Norwegian folk song and game https://itunes.apple.com/us/album/tyven-tyven/id399319557?i=399319667

"Escravos de Jó," Dino Lingo, iTunes, Brazilian children's game https://itunes.apple.com/us/album/escravos-de-j%C3%B3/id637835895?i=637836029

"March of the Belgian Paratroopers," Eastern Wind Symphony, iTunes, European march for wind ensemble instrumentation https://itunes.apple.com/us/album/march-of-the-belgian-paratroopers/id490516908?i=490517282

"Australia: Morning Star, Pigeon and Rain Songs," Musical Sources, Smithsonian Folkways, *didjeridu* of indigenous Australia https://folkways.si.edu/australia-morning-star-pigeon-and-rain-songs-excerpt/music/track/smithsonian

"Cuadro Flamenco," Spain: Flamenco Music of Andalusia, Smithsonian Folkways, flamenco music of the Andalusian region of Spain https://folkways.si.edu/cuadro-flamenco/world/music/track/smithsonian

4

Performing World Music

The last morning of music camp begins with a very different energy than any other day—today is the day 15 campers, ages 4 through 6, will share their "world music" in performance for their families and friends. Throughout the week, the pageant has generated much excitement in the young children, from rehearsing, to exploring the performance space, to learning what color the camp t-shirt would be, and even to learning that a cheese stick would be the pre-pageant snack! These campers spent the first four days of the week traveling around the musical world, filling their homemade passports with stamps to acknowledge their various musical engagements.

Fifteen campers, in their matching lime green t-shirts, are lined up at the back of a bright, orange-carpeted church sanctuary. They are giggling and wiggling, for now is the time they perform! Led by their teacher, all 15 little ones proceed happily to the front of the sanctuary, up one step, then another, to line up and finally face their parents, siblings, grandparents, babysitters, friends, and other loved ones. With small laminated paper airplanes colored by the campers themselves, and paper bags representing suitcases for travel, the pageant commences with a song, easily customizable to various global locales through the use of drums, gongs, claves, and body percussion:

> *Around the world we go,*
> *Hearing new music, meeting new friends.*
> *All sorts of new things to know,*
> *Let's see where our journey ends.*

The campers' first stop in the program is Japan, where they perform a traditional children's song about an expressive frog, called "Kaeru No Uta." The audience is invited to guess which animal the song might be describing. After a few failed guesses, the children pull frog finger puppets out of their bags to reveal the true answer, which presses them to sing with greater exuberance than earlier.

Next on the program's itinerary is a trip to the Andes mountains. The children quickly form a circle and perform a traditional dance to a recording of the tune "Viva Jujuy" featuring beautiful singing, flutes, and the lute with the armadillo body known as the charango. They sing with the recording, just to maintain the flavor of the instruments. Their circle undulates in and out, rotates around, and even has the performers spinning gently in place. As the dance comes to a close, the campers are ready for a trip to Tanzania and a quick stretch to the song "Simama Kaa," and the little ones are moving up and down as they sing, adding jumps to the cadences.

Following the quick movement break, the campers depart for a tropical locale, arriving in Hawai'i. What better way to learn about Hawaiian culture than to learn about the Hawaiian language? The campers surprise their families with an expertly performed rendition of "Mele Pi'āpa," the Hawaiian alphabet song. Their knowledge of Hawaiian vowels, consonants, and even the 'okina, or glottal stop, is quite impressive. Carefully positioned hand drums are grasped by the children in preparation for their next stop in Ghana. While older children might know the popular West African tune "Sansa Kroma" as a passing game, these little ones are preparing their rhythmic sensibilities by performing the song with a steady beat tapped on the drums.

The time has come for the pageant to end. As the campers arrive back safely in America from their global tour, they pull red, white, and blue scarves from their bags for free movement to a recording of "Stars and Stripes Forever!" Theirs was a journey of considerable diversity in which the young children were able to demonstrate just how capable they are when it comes to engagement with and performance of the world's musical cultures.

Early Childhood on Stage: Performing World Music

The prior vignette tells of the culmination of a weeklong summer music camp facilitated for children 4 to 6 years of age. Each day-camp session featured a variety of activities that were aimed at opening their minds to the world's peoples and that were unified by the theme of exploring the world's musical cultures in a child-friendly way. Closing the camp with a short performance of a selection of music they learned that week seemed a natural way to bring a sense of accomplishment and completion to the young campers while providing them with an opportunity to share with their parents and caregivers all they had achieved throughout the week. As preparations were made during the days of camp, the children's excitement built exponentially until they were almost ready to explode with the excitement of sharing what they had learned of the world.

Music is a performing art, one that thrives in community and is meant to be shared with others. Why not allow young children the experience to sing, play, and dance? Young children are compelled to share and to be observed—many times a committed caregiver is perched on a playground watching a little one slide and swing to shouts of "watch me!" They are already natural performers and can present their musical knowledge and skill in a variety of capacities with tremendous enthusiasm.

A consideration in moving forward with performances of music of the world's cultures in the early childhood setting can and should be collaboration. Music teachers, classroom teachers, daycare providers, parents, and siblings can all contribute to the performing opportunities that little ones might enjoy. Music teachers and classroom teachers might consider topics of interest and together craft a cross-curricular pageant that showcases a fusion of academic and artistic knowledge. Parents, caregivers, and family members can be involved, not just as audience members, but as contributors, to performances in hands-on ways by sharing of their family's musical and cultural knowledge. Just as children's musical engagement and skill emerge organically, so might the combined efforts of important figures in children's lives organically combine to create a meaningful musical performing experience. Ahead are a variety of ways to conceptualize and organize early childhood musical performances as well as concrete suggestions for programming.

The "Playformance"

A play on the word "performance," the concept "playformance" is a compelling one for young children. In this type of performance, the audience members are invited to participate—to sing along, to move and dance, to join with the children as they share their musicking. This model is one that is ideal for young children as it removes the pressure of a traditional style of performance in which the audience is separate both in space and behavior. Instead, people come together in the communal spirit inherent in the act of making music. As pictured in Figure 4.1, the playformance may involve an audience of parents and caregivers, or, perhaps, sharing with other groups of children. In any manifestation, the thrust of the event is to showcase young children's singing, movement, instrument playing, storytelling, and creativity in a safe way.

Figure 4.1 Children and families in a participatory playformance

Kindergartners can engage their upper elementary school "book buddies" in these events, and preschool classes can share their music with other groups of children in their daycare facility. These invested audience members may participate with the performers by joining in with the chanting rhythmic patterns, creating body percussion sounds, participating in free movement, or simply by singing along. The beauty of the playformance is its malleability and potential to take on myriad forms that suit children, families, and teachers.

The School Program

Young children in pre-Kindergarten, Kindergarten, or first grade may find themselves included in a larger elementary school setting, perhaps in a pre-K–5 or pre-K–8 type of configuration. In many of these school settings, school music performances take place multiple times throughout the school year, such as winter holidays, Music in Our Schools Month (sponsored by the National Association for Music Education), or a spring showcase. In this situation, young children might find themselves part of a larger program, performing only a small piece of the overall musical presentation. When this is the case, it is best to have the youngest children perform first while they are still fresh and attentive, at the start of a longer program, after which they can join their parents and families in the audience. This performing scenario can be immensely beneficial to little ones as they see a plethora of musical role models unfold before them—they even latch on to the music performed by older children and appropriate that for themselves, hopping into music class with requests to learn more of what their older counterparts were able to perform. Young children may even be called upon to present an entire formal performance by themselves, as in the following description.

In the late days of May, thoughts of graduation are in the air—not just high school and college graduates, but graduation by 5- and 6-year-old Kindergarten children from what is probably their first year of formal education into the elementary "grades." In both music class and homeroom, the Kindergartners and their teachers have worked hard to prepare a program of songs, speech pieces, and movement, along with the careful rehearsal of graduation logistics of processionals, recessionals, and the navigating of the quickest path to the spot where diplomas are distributed. These are sizable tasks for little ones!

At last it is graduation day! Dressed in their finery, 48 Kindergartners line up at the back of the auditorium where their ceremony is being held. The music teacher is poised at the front of the hall and begins Elgar's "Pomp and Circumstance" on the piano. The children take this cue to begin processing to their spots in the front. After several brief pauses to wave at family members, the Kindergarteners arrive at their places. They proceed with their program featuring a selection of songs including an African American spiritual, a Hungarian song with motions about a silly bear, and even their most favorite goodbye song, a Spanish-Cuban song from music class. They performed these with minimal assistance (just accompaniment from the music teacher) to great acclaim from their families and teachers. Their names are then called to receive their diplomas. A few words of closure and encouragement are spoken and then the Kindergartners recess to the South African tune of "Siyahamba."

The Team Effort

Consideration of performing music in the early childhood years might beg the question, "Can little kids really *do* that?" Developmental characteristics of children are most certainly considered in this context. Perhaps a particular group of children might not have the appropriate tools or skills to perform anything extensive yet. The creative teacher can still craft a musical performance that is appropriate, empowering, and fun. The teacher may join in a team effort with little ones, providing a narrative, or story, or some other unifying thread for children to respond to. Perhaps children and audience members respond together. Take the example of a Thanksgiving musical performance of 2- and 3-year-olds in which the children provided just a simple sung response. In the weeks prior to Thanksgiving, the music teacher surveyed the children, inquiring, "What are you thankful for?" A motley assortment of responses issued forth, addressing everything from family, to jumping in leaves, to pumpkins, markers, bracelets, grapes, and crayons. The teacher was then able read aloud the children's contributions, "We are thankful for _______," while the children chimed in with a response of "We are thankful" sung on the intervals of sol, mi, la, sol, mi. To accompany this ubiquitous childhood musical interval found in cultures across the entire world, a global spin on this sequence features the inclusion of multiple languages. Teachers may customize the languages included to reflect the languages spoken in the surrounding community. This particular performance may serve as a model of intentionally including the children's thoughts and input while inviting them to contribute a simple yet meaningful musical offering.

Call and response songs may extend this paradigm further, with the teacher providing the call and young children chiming in with a repeated response. The Ghanaian children's song "Kye Kye Kule" (Figure 4.2) is a perfect example of the team effort that can occur between a teacher and her children while engaging with the world's musical cultures. The teacher sings the initial call and models the motions, while the children simply respond back. This format eliminates the possibility of memory lapses and may ease performance anxiety as children know they will have their teacher to depend upon. Figure 4.3 pictures children engaging in this performance format while the teacher (off-stage) leads the call and response. An extra participatory twist may come into the mix if audience members are invited to join in the responses.

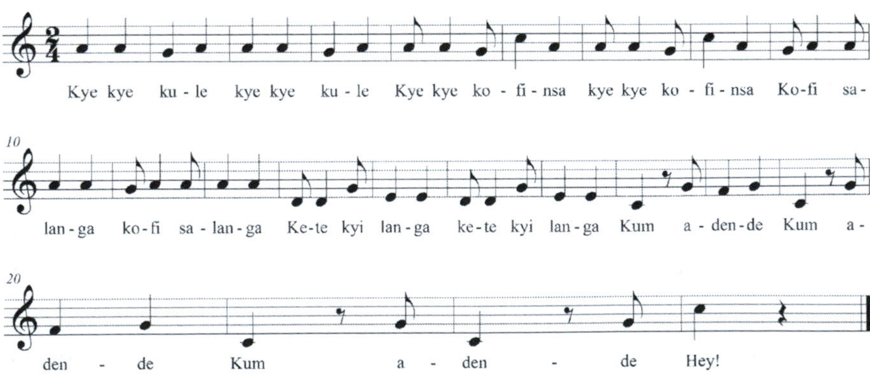

Figure 4.2 Notation for "Kye Kye Kule"

Figure 4.3 Diligently preparing for an upcoming performance

Age-Appropriate Performances: Strategies for Success

Young children are adept at living in the present moment, that is, they focus on the "now," a characteristic that might present a challenge in preparing performances in which the reward of sharing is far off in the future. Knowing one's learners in terms of developmental characteristics is of utmost importance to teachers, as some prefer the limelight and leadership while others are more comfortable following or singing in a circle facing one another rather than standing in lines that face the audience. Importantly, intensive rehearsals for a "perfect performance" are not going to be in the realm of what is appropriate for early childhood. As well, lengthy, focused performances are out of line for little ones (both in terms of their own endurances as singers, players, and dancers, as well as their capacity to listen and watch others perform). Their performance preparation should come in limited doses, with the teacher reading the children to know when the threshold of attention and focus has passed. Neither should their performances be intensive and lengthy, but, rather, framed playfully. Just as young children are high-energy beings, their performances should be planned and implemented to capitalize on these assets.

While preparing for a performance, it is helpful to be as concrete as possible, appealing to the senses of sight, sound, and touch. When possible, the children should be able to rehearse in the space where the performance will take place—this eliminates any surprises and discomfort that may arise from entering new spaces. They should experience what it is like to walk into the performing space, locate their spot, move from one activity to the next, and know what to do at the culmination of the performance. Further, it is wise to engage children in some storytelling and questioning about the performance process, posing prompts and queries like, "Is it safe to run off the stage in the middle of a song?" or "Should you be touching your neighbor when we are singing?" or "Show me how to stand during a performance." Will a performance with early childhood learners be perfect and polished? Probably not, but that is what makes a performance of this age group so endearing.

Sometimes young children prepare well in advance of the performance but are overcome with stage fright when it comes time to share. Many a time a parent has approached a teacher to reveal a child's performance anxiety, or the child himself might express a fear of performing in public. This is all helpful information as the teacher can plan an appropriate response. Perhaps a helper is available to sit with a child who is uncomfortable in the performance and needs to observe from the sidelines. Perhaps the teacher can craft a discussion session in which children are invited to voice their fears about performing. In this case, the teacher might frequently find that other children jump in to support their anxious peers with tales of how they survived violin recitals or sharing a treasured object with their classmates in show-and-tell. Forcing young children to perform is not developmentally appropriate and could be detrimental to their desire to pursue music further. The following story highlights an instance where the last-minute anxiety of performing for an audience proved to be a challenge for a young child.

The twin girls are so alike in many aspects, and not just in their looks. They are enthusiastic contributors to music class, participating nicely in a variety of activities, bubbly and vivacious in nature. The twin girls are alike until the day of the music class playformance. The classroom is prepared for the playformance: half open for the children to perform and half filled with rows of padded chairs for parents and caregivers to sit and enjoy the music. The children are lined up outside the classroom door, ready to make their entrance. The children begin to file in—one twin heads to the front of the room, ready to sing and dance, while the other takes one glimpse of the crowd gathered and makes a beeline for the bench on the periphery of the room. There she stays planted with a high school–age helper until the culmination of the playformance. After the event, she is still praised for her hard work in preparing all the songs and movements with her friends!

Thematic Suggestions for Early Childhood World Music Performances

Getting started with preparing a performance of world music with young children can be as simple as determining a theme that will unify the selections to be rehearsed and shared. Perhaps a global overview might be pursued, featuring selections from many of the world's cultures. Or, one might wish to highlight a particular region of the world, such as Eastern Europe, West Africa, the Pacific Islands, or Southeast Asia, or a particular culture-sharing group, such as traditional Andean peoples or Aboriginal Australians. The cultures represented by the children may guide this choice (either highlighting the children's cultural origins or intentionally exposing them to something new), as well as access to community experts and culture-bearers who can engage and share with the children. World instruments might serve as a unifying agent, as well. For example, a program revolving around flutes of the world might feature children singing and moving to an Andean panpipe tune, an American Revolutionary War era fife melody, and a Japanese *shakuhachi* piece. World percussion might present a potential strand, with many of the world's musical cultures featuring various shakers and drums that are easily accessible to young children.

Teachers have a responsibility to not just instruct young children in the doing of music, but also to educate audience members about the diversity of music they hear in these performance contexts. Providing context for each musical culture represented brings the parents and caregivers more completely into the musical moments, perhaps even providing points of departure for further discussion with their children. All involved benefit from the teacher's model of care and attention to the origins of world music expressions and practices, taking careful note that music comes from important people and places. Just because a performance is for young children does not mean that the music should be oversimplified or infantile—little ones are capable of substantive musicking deserving of sharing. Consider the following vignette.

Mr. James had prepared his students for many weeks leading up to the spring concert which had just come to a close. Among the pieces performed were a Hawaiian pule, a French folk tune, a polyrhythmic West African drumming session, a Native American canoe song, and even some pop and jazz. Following the concert, a parent approached Mr. James. "Fantastic performance, Mr. James!" the mother squealed. "The kids did a great job singing—and the music you chose was actually interesting to listen to! Thanks!" Mr. James thanked the parent for her kind feedback, laughing to himself that, yes, of course, children are capable of making music that is interesting to listen to!

Young children live in themed worlds with their television cartoon themed bedroom sets, their storybook character lunch boxes, and thematically decorated classrooms and units of study in childcare and school settings. Many of these themes arise from the academic curricula guiding the work of teachers and children in this setting or simply from the interests common to children of this age group. The following are posited as compelling themes around which to craft performances of early childhood world music, accompanied by sample programs that teachers may wish to implement as written or adapted to suit the needs of their children.

Animals

Many young children are very enthusiastic about animals! (And many teachers, as well!) There are a wealth of animal-themed tunes from the world over that young children can perform with ease. The Japanese children's song about frogs, "Kaeru No Uta," is easily grasped by little ones and can be connected to other frog songs and stories. The American folk classic "John the Rabbit" (Figure 4.4) makes a wonderful opportunity for solo singing on the "oh yes" parts and can even lead to some improvisatory work regarding what garden delights John the Rabbit will be sneaking next. Another American folk classic is "Bought Me a Cat" (featured in Chapter 3), where, again, children might invent and perform their own verses with animals and sounds of their choosing (Figure 4.5). Very young children in their toddler years might simply make the animal sounds and accompany the animal names with sign language. The Balinese children's

Figure 4.4 Notation for "John the Rabbit"

Figure 4.5 Notation for "Bought Me a Cat"

song "Meong Meong" draws children in with the idea of a cat-and-mouse chase. The steelpan selection "Coqui" (Chapter 5) could round out an animal-themed performance with movement and vocal improvisations.

Nature

The Learning Pathway featuring the Chinese song "Moli Hua" (Figure 4.6) is a perfect example of bringing the World Music Pedagogy process into the performance realm. Through the Attentive Listening, Engaged Listening, and Enactive Listening steps, children can be prepared to perform the melody or to move Eurhythmically to the music, interpreting the gentle unfurling and retreat of the jasmine blossom. Likewise, the Learning Pathway selection of "Anoai" might feature young children performing the *'uli 'uli* patterns on shakers, interpreting the gentle falling of rain. Children might also enjoy Ladysmith Black Mambazo's "Rain, Rain, Beautiful Rain" (for further information, see Chapter 6), where they might perform motions to mimic the water cycle in this piece that celebrates life-giving precipitation.

Figure 4.6 Notation for "Moli Hua"

Sharing and Community

Many early childhood curricula give attention to the importance of community, of sharing and being a good citizen of the classroom and the world outside the doors of school. A musical performance could very well be organized around this important theme. For example, "Viva Jujuy," an Andean tune featured in Chapter 6, speaks to the importance of loving one's homeland and, in turn, loving those with whom home is shared. Additionally, the traditional Andean cultures are focused on the importance of community, of all sharing in the making of music together regardless of skill level. Bringing "Viva Jujuy" into the performance realm can be a wonderful opportunity for early childhood learners to share a musical manifestation of community and sharing. The performance may be extended with the Andean children's song and game "Juego Chirimbolo," a fun game that children can sing, play, and perform together. The Learning Pathway featuring the Tera xylophone of Nigeria might be an addition to this sharing and community theme as many West African xylophones are played in pairs or groups. Children might perform on Orff barred percussion, sharing a modified version of this piece as an example of musical community.

Letters and Numbers

Literacy, math skills, and other childhood basics come into play in the early childhood world. The Letter of the Week or Number of the Week is a frequent fixture in early childhood settings—children delight in spotting their special letter or digit out in the world! The possibilities are endless for planning a performance around the letters and numbers! A Letter "M" program might feature *mbira* music, maracas, marches, and movement (see *mbira* lesson from Chapter 5, march lesson from chapter 3). A Letter "S" program might feature *shakuhachi* music, steelpan, shakers, singing, and stomping (see steelpan lesson from Chapter 5, elephant lesson from Chapter 2). A letter "D" program could feature drums, dancing, dynamics, and the *didjeridu*. Children might make some connections to math skills with a number-themed pageant that could relate to the meters of the pieces featured or patterns played on instruments or sung.

Figure 4.7 Hawaiian color song—translation: red, yellow, purple, blue, black, pink, white, gray, green

Colors

A basic and necessary aspect of the early childhood curriculum, colors and visual art may make up the foundation for an early childhood music performance. There are many cultures from around the world that have songs that help young children learn their colors, for example, the Hawaiian color song in Figure 4.7. Add into the mix a beautiful dance to the Spring Festival of Colors piece (see Chapter 2) and the American folk tune "Black Snake" and a teacher is well underway with crafting a color-themed program.

The Five Senses

In the early childhood years, little ones learn about themselves and how they interact with the world. Engaging their five senses is a great way for young children to learn, exploring the world through sight, sound, touch, taste, and smell. Children can put their knowledge of the five senses to work in a musical presentation that celebrates this aspect of human life. While the entire performance would certainly qualify for the sense of hearing, teachers and students can get creative with the other four. Perhaps a movement piece to "Moli Hua" factors into the scene, with the gentle and lilting melody inspiring and insinuating something soft to touch. A dance with colorful scarves, ribbons, or other props might awaken the sense of sight. Playing instruments to the "Anoai" hula mele chant might inspire the audience to recall the smell of rain as it falls and wets the earth. The sense of taste would be best engaged with a celebration of sweet global treats after the show like pan dulce, baklava, or mochi!

Fables and Nursery Rhymes

Storytelling is most certainly a staple of childhood, in both oral and written forms. The fables, fairy tales, and nursery rhymes that capture the imaginations of children might serve well as the basis for a performance of the world's musical cultures. Many nursery rhymes have lovely rhythmic sensibilities that children latch onto and chant with ease. Add in some melodic or rhythmic instruments for accompaniment or improvisation and a performance is in the works. A teacher might select various parts of the world to represent and collect stories and rhymes from print resources or culture-bearers to string together for rehearsal and performance. *The Singing Sack* by Helen East can be a good resource to launch a storytelling program.

Children's Literature

The previous program development idea might serve as a launch pad for a more detailed performance of a single story. Many children's books are ripe with opportunities to be musical—rhyming couplets to chant, repeating phrases to sing, words that invite vocal exploration, and so forth. A teacher could easily adapt a children's story for performative use. Take, for example, the classic childhood story of *The Very Hungry Caterpillar* by Eric Carle. This story has been translated into many languages and has been enjoyed by children the world over. In this tale, a small caterpillar becomes very hungry and eats many different fruits (and eventually a whole feast) in preparation for his time to build a chrysalis and transform into a beautiful butterfly. Perhaps each of these fruits might be "performed" by the children in some capacity, each represented by a unique global instrument or a different cultural groove such as the *cha cha cha* of "Oye Como Va" or an improvisatory jam to "Tutuki" (both found in chapter 5). A final butterfly dance may be presented at the end of the program, a Eurythmic dance to the music of the teacher's culture of choice. The aforementioned story is just an example—the world of children's literature is a treasure chest of many tales that can be adapted for early childhood music performance.

Performance of People

A perfect point of departure for early childhood musical performance is people! Music is a human art form, intricately woven into the lifeways and traditions of people around the world. Starting with the people themselves makes sense, then, as a way to explore musical performance. For example, a program or pageant might celebrate a local cultural presence through singing and dance. Lithuanian folk dance, African American spirituals, Balinese gamelan, South American folk tunes, North Indian classical music, and more could both celebrate local culture while providing a platform for children to sing, move, play, and dance. Culture-bearers from the surrounding community are an excellent resource—they bring with them first-hand knowledge of their context and musical traditions, engaging young children in a level of authenticity that their teachers may not be able to provide. Parents, grandparents, aunts, uncles, caregivers, and community members may all play a role in introducing young children to the ways in which people across the globe make music and make meaning of music. Children themselves are people, too, and a program or pageant might very well revolve around their choices of music, stories, dances, and speech pieces that they have experienced throughout their school and music encounters.

Holidays and Celebrations

Many early childhood learning centers or Kindergarten and first grade music classes put on short performances in celebration of various holidays and traditions around the world. The bright lights and colors of Diwali, the prayerful lighting of candles during Chanukah, and the reflective and unifying themes of Kwanzaa all make compelling points of departure for early childhood musical sharing. The many and varied Christmas traditions around the world including Las Posadas might appeal to children and their families while the exciting music and dance traditions of Chinese New Year present opportunities to wish one another good fortune for the coming year. Secular holidays celebrating national days of remembrance can reflect musical traditions of many locales. Perhaps a performance might focus on one holiday celebration or might integrate many in an all-inclusive showcase of musical celebrations of many peoples. Chapter 6 offers a few points of departure for integrating songs of Chanukah, Las Posadas, and Chinese New Year into the early childhood curriculum which can then, most certainly, be shared as part of a public performance.

Sample Performance Programs

Again, just getting started might be challenging for teachers, but once they do, the possibilities are endless! The following sample programs are offered as points of departure for engaging children in the public sharing of their musical gems. Teachers of young children should carefully assess their students' musical and social comfort levels prior to implementing any performances or playformances, ensuring that the experience is meaningful and positive.

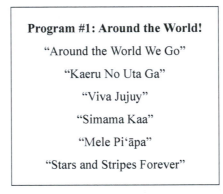

Program #1: Around the World!

"Around the World We Go"

"Kaeru No Uta Ga"

"Viva Jujuy"

"Simama Kaa"

"Mele Pi'āpa"

"Stars and Stripes Forever"

In a globally oriented program of the sort described in the opening vignette, children from ages 4 to 7 are able to share musical selections from around the world in a variety of different modes. The "Around the World We Go" song (Figure 4.8) is one musical way for kicking off the performance and can also serve as a unifying thread by being performed before each new "place" visited by the children. In this program, young children are able to demonstrate their singing skills in the opening number as well as in "Kaeru No Uta Ga" (Figure 4.9), "Simama Kaa" (Figure 4.11) and "Mele Pi'āpa" (Ho'omāka'ika'i Staff, 2007). The may showcase their Eurhythmic movement skills in a choreographed manner in the Andean folk dance, "Viva Jujuy" (Figure 4.10), and their improvisatory movement skills through a scarf dance to "Stars and Stripes Forever." Further additions to this program might be inviting children to create paper airplanes to move about during the "Around the World" song, or even crafting a large airplane out of foam core board where children can peek their faces through the plane windows. This program is one that children love to share and families love to view!

A - round the world we go, hear-ing new mu - sic, meet-ing new friends. All
sorts of new things to know, let's see where our jour - ney ends.

Figure 4.8 Notation for "Around the World We Go"

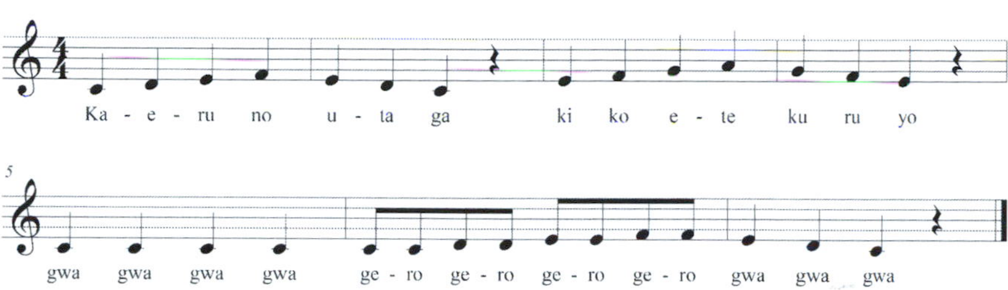
Ka - e - ru no u - ta ga ki ko e - te ku ru yo
gwa gwa gwa gwa ge - ro ge - ro ge - ro ge - ro gwa gwa gwa

Figure 4.9 Notation for "Kaeru No Uta Ga"

Vi-va Ju-juy Vi-va la pu-na Vi-va mi'a-ma - da Vi-van los cerr-os pin-ta-rra-jea-dos
de mi que - bra - da de mi que - bra - da Hu-ma - hua - que - na
No te se - par - es de mis a - mor - es Tu'e - res mi due - na.

Figure 4.10 Notation for "Viva Jujuy"

Si - ma - ma kaa si - ma - ma kaa ru-ka ru-ka ru-ka si - ma-ma kaa

Figure 4.11 Notation for "Simama Kaa"

Program #2: Sounds of our Natural World

The Rainforest—"Rain, Rain"

The Mountains—"Viva Jujuy

The Ocean—"E Ke Akua"

The Forest—"The Tree Song"

The Finale—"Moli Hua"

The Sounds of our Natural World Pageant is one that children and families alike find compelling through the opportunities to explore different biomes and landscapes of the world through multicultural musics that reflect each area. Designed for 4- to 6-year-olds, the program begins with a first stop in the rainforest. This visit features a very simple tune, "Rain, Rain," that serves as an A Section followed by a body percussion rainstorm in the B Section (Figures 4.12 and 4.13). Children may create their "storm" by first snapping fingers for gentle rain, rubbing palms together for moderate rain, patting legs for heavy rain, and finally stomping feet to symbolize a thunderous downpour. Little ones delight in creating their storms! A shake of a thunder tube makes a lively and unexpected conclusion to this piece. Visiting the mountains is another great way to incorporate the traditional Andean folk dance of "Viva Jujuy." It is especially compelling to discuss the text of this tune as a love song to one's mountainous homeland. A visit to the ocean and beach environment is not complete without a traditional Hawaiian pule, "E Ke Akua" (Figure 4.14), which children can easily sing accompanied by a few gentle chords strummed on the ukulele. The New England Dancing Masters book *Down in the Valley* features "The Tree Song," a perfect tune for a visit to the forest. A musical story of the various phases a deciduous tree progresses through over the course of the four seasons, children fall in love with this tune and make it special and memorable with motions and their very best singing. Eurhythmic movement with scarves to "Moli Hua" makes a visually satisfying conclusion to this program, with children's jasmine "petals" unfolding during the night and contracting during the day.

Program #3: The Magnificent, Musical M!

Making Music with Maracas—"Oye Como Va"

Marching—"The March of the Belgian Paratroopers"

Mbira Magic—"Taireva"

Movement—"Moli Hua"

Figure 4.12 Notation for "Rain, Rain"

- Snap fingers gently
- Rub hands together
- Pat lap quickly, alternating hands
- Stomp feet to simulate thunder
- Cease Body Percussion
- Sing "Rain, Rain"
- Repeat Body Percussion Sequence and "Rain, Rain" as desired

Figure 4.13 Rainstorm body percussion sequence

Figure 4.14 Notation for "E Ke Akua"

As previously mentioned, many early childhood curricula address the basics of language, including learning the alphabet and other related literacy skills. This program offers a refreshing point of departure using the letter "M" as a unifying thread, showcasing the musical and linguistic skills of 4- to 7-year-olds. Preparations leading up to the performance might include exploration of this letter and its corresponding sound and the myriad places it might be found. This program could feature children making a grand entrance to "Oye Como Va," playing some basic rhythms on their maracas as they process to the front of the performance area. They may follow up with a march, performed as a movement ensemble with a parachute to the tune of "The March of the Belgian Paratroopers" (see Chapter 3). The *mbira* tune "Taireva," found in Chapter 5, presents children with an opportunity to improvise to the *mbira* and even craft and play their own homemade version. The program might conclude with movement to "Moli Hua" or another piece that fills out the cultures represented and modes of musicking found throughout.

Teacher Feature: Ms. Grace Watson-Martin

Grace Watson-Martin Facilitating a Drumming Activity

Ms. Grace Watson-Martin is a new teacher and an accomplished vocalist who has decided to dedicate her teaching path to young children in elementary school settings. Ms. Watson-Martin has had many formative experiences in her pre-service training that led to her desire to work with young children, including working with 4-year-olds in a campus daycare and working with Kindergartners as a camp counselor. Following those foundational encounters, she "fell in love with the chaos of little children and how wonderful they are . . . I love how honest they are whether good or bad. I love how simple the world is to them." Ms. Watson-Martin serves as an exemplary model to new teachers who may be interested in exploring the many facets of World Music Pedagogy. Her world music interests include the Zuni people of New Mexico and traditional musics of the Peruvian Andes mountains.

Q: Can you describe your involvement with early childhood music, birth through Kindergarten?

A: My first experience was working at the [campus daycare] where we got to work with 4-year-olds in music immersion. After that class, I really fell in love with the little ones, so I took a [summer] job as a day-camp counselor for Kindergartners. I found that general music is really what I love to do, especially with the little guys. I find that they fit my demeanor.

Q: Can you tell me a little bit about your philosophy of listening to music in this age range?
A: Little ones are able to be open to so many things at that age, so I think it's important that they get a variety of music to listen to. I know when I was a child, I listened to the radio, but my parents also established classical music [in my life], and I think that has helped me get to where I am as an adult. As music educators [we need to remember that] not all children get that at home. It's important that we let them experience classical music, pop music, multicultural music, a little bit of everything, because the more that's ingrained in them, the more an understanding and respect will be there in them for music and people as they get older.

Q: What world cultures are of interest to you, and how do you incorporate musical examples from these cultures?
A: Zuni culture was one I implemented in my field experience. I went on a trip to New Mexico as a child and really fell in love with the Native American pueblos there. That's part of the reason I looked into that culture. I just think it's very beautiful, very to the earth. I also had the opportunity to visit Peru. I'm currently looking into Peruvian culture. I'm very passionate about Andes music.

Q: You have developed your interests in Zuni culture and Peruvian culture by going there, traveling, seeing things in person. How are you translating these experiences into pedagogical approaches and materials?
A: The current district where I am teaching has a lot of Latino children who attend there. Even though Peruvian culture might not be their culture, the Spanish language of many Peruvian pieces connects with students. When I teach Peruvian songs, some children will say, "I understand what you said!" without the translation because they speak Spanish. Those are just the little things that make a difference. Other children, they want to learn another language, they want to learn about other cultures, and when they see other children in the class who are really passionate about it, it creates a really great learning environment.

Q: Could you tell me about your Zuni culture unit that you created? What was it like to get young children involved in singing, dancing, and doing things they have never tried before?
A: The started off with listening to a Zuni harvest dance. It's an interesting piece of music because it's kind of mixed meter, the range is wide, the intervals are less commonly heard [by American school children]. It was interesting when I was playing the music to watch children's facial expressions. They seemed very intrigued. After they learned how to sing it, we put some drumming with it. After we got that, we added a dance. I did simplify [the dance] for [younger children] but I did try to keep the basics elements of using shakers and the various body movements in order to keep it as culturally appropriate as possible while still allowing [young children] to have that experience.

Q: What materials did you use to help you launch this lesson?
A: Smithsonian Folkways was helpful. I read extensively about the Zuni people and reviewed YouTube videos of Zuni people dancing, singing, performing ceremonies, things like that. I wanted to get a taste of what Zuni culture is about and also to take

the time to think about it pedagogically in terms of how to facilitate learning for young children.

Q: So, you wanted to learn more about the Zuni culture, but also acknowledging that you are seeing it through your own cultural lens?
A: I had to realize that I'm not Zuni. Everyone has initial judgments when they see [a new kind of music], and I wanted to make sure I spoke to those judgments to myself. Considering, "Why do I think that way?" so that I wouldn't bring my incorrect judgements into the classroom. Or, if these ideas did come up in the classroom, I would have a way to counter these [potentially disrespectful comments]. I had already thought through it.

Q: Do you have any advice for fellow new music teachers to get started with World Music Pedagogy with early childhood?
A: I have friendly mentors who are oriented toward the world's musical cultures, so they are great resources. I'd recommend that new teachers reach out to a mentor teacher, possibly even a friend who is well versed in a particular culture. For my Peruvian projects—my mom is from Peru, so I talk to her a lot! I'd recommend that teachers learn to recognize their own biases, and that when they teach of other cultures, that they are enthusiastic about these cultures. Always be uplifting, and check with resources, including mentors, to make sure what you are doing is appropriate.

Q: Any final bits of wisdom for new teachers like yourself who are seeking to incorporate World Music Pedagogy into their classrooms?
A: I love to travel. If teachers have the opportunity to go somewhere, they should really invest in doing so. Music is a part of the cultures to travel to, just as much as are language, ceremonies, and other traditions. Also, teachers can learn to get out of their comfort zones every now and then. Every so often I try to learn a new [to me] culture, and I listen to and view the music. Teachers need to keep their ears open, because if they're not, who else is going to do that for the children?

Care, Caution, and Conclusions

It warrants repeating that early childhood music is an informal affair. Young children participate in their musical environments as they are ready, with emergent skills such as use of singing voice or keeping a steady beat. Some young children need time to observe and absorb and might not be ready to jump in and be outwardly musical in a public performance setting. Repertoire should be carefully selected to ensure developmental appropriateness as well as a balance of world cultures represented. The facilitation of performances needs to be navigated carefully so as not to scare or overwhelm young children or stray into developmentally inappropriate teaching practices. Child-friendly performances may take on the form of the "playformance," where audience members are invited to share in the active musicking, thereby taking a bit of pressure off the children. Further, themes engaging to early childhood can help teachers craft compelling programs that children will enjoy performing. When implemented thoughtfully, performances of early childhood music learners are entirely possible—and adorable!

References

Carle, E. (1969). *The very hungry caterpillar*. New York, NY: Putnam.

Davis, A. & Amidon, P. (2000). *Down in the valley: More great singing games for children*. Brattleboro, VT: New England Dancing Masters.

East, H. (1989). *The singing sack: 28 song-stories from around the world*. London, UK: A & C Black.

Ho'omāka'ika'i Staff. (2007). *Explorations! Ho'omāka'ika'i* (4th Ed.). Honolulu, HI: Kamehameha Schools Press.

Listening Episodes—Learning Pathways

"Anoai," Jacob Feuerring with Tom Hiona, Smithsonian Folkways, *hula kahiko* featuring *'uli 'uli* gourd rattles www.folkways.si.edu/hawaiian-dancers-male-singer/anoai-hula-uliuli/hawaii/music/track/smithsonian

"Moli Hua," Crystal Children's Choir & Karl Chang, iTunes, choral arrangement of traditional Chinese melody https://itunes.apple.com/WebObjects/MZStore.woa/wa/viewCollaboration?cc=us&ids=431607970-431607973

Tera Xylophone," Music from the Villages of Northeastern Nigeria, "Smithsonian Folkways, traditional xylophones of West Africa www.folkways.si.edu/music-of-the-tera-people-tera-xylophone-music/world/music/track/smithsonian

Listening Episode

"Stars and Stripes Forever," John Philip Sousa, iTunes https://itunes.apple.com/us/album/stars-and-stripes-forever/id317375461

5

Creating World Music

One might wonder what on earth babies and toddlers can do in a music class. The infants and toddlers in today's childcare center music class are ready to demonstrate that they can do quite a lot! Various staff members and some parents may join in the fun, aligning their breaks from the neighboring businesses with the daycare music time, enjoying a few musical moments with their children. A circle of sorts is formed, and baby-safe shakers are distributed. The only thing more fun than shaking the instruments is tasting them!

The children bask in their musical environment—perhaps they are not able to sing along yet or move in a perfectly coordinated way, but they are there, soaking up every pitch and rhythm, and seeing and hearing models of the caregivers in their lives purposefully engaging in music. Their eyes dart from here to there, sensing sounds and looking for their sources. Their heads bob, arms wave up and down, their torsos and legs bouncing in the uninhibited way only early childhood learners can. They listen and watch, frequently making use of the same manipulatives as their older counterparts—scarves flail and wave, finger puppets sail about (with an occasional tasting as they bring the soft and colorful felt figures to their mouths), and instruments are explored in their tiny hands.

After much singing, moving, storytelling, and dancing, it is time for one of the babies' most favorite activities—Baby Bucket Band! A teacher-created activity, Baby Bucket Band (Figure 5.1) features a variety of household objects—small buckets, plastic mixing spoons, plastic bottles of varying sizes filled with rice or beans or lentils, bowls, and more. A perfect opportunity to incorporate some of the soundscapes of the world, some background music is selected and played, and the teacher tips over the storage container and allows the contents to spill onto the floor in front of the children. As if operating on instinct, no directions needed, the children scoot, crawl, and toddle over to the pile of homemade sound-makers. They explore, shake, swirl, roll, toss, bang, slam, and wiggle with their implements, finding the sounds

Figure 5.1 Infants engaging with baby bucket band homemade instruments

and combinations they like best. Without adult guidance, they match up the spoons and buckets and drum away happily. They are in control of the sounds they choose and what and how they create—an exciting prospect for those still in diapers!

Laying the Groundwork for Composition and Improvisation

Creativity is at the core of early childhood, with so many new things to explore and investigate. Cultivating curious, creative learners is embedded within many approaches to early childhood education, such as the Montessori approach, providing children with the time, space, and tools to experiment, problem-solve, and simply try new things. Musical creativity comes naturally to young children. From the undulating coos and babbles of infancy to the vocalizations, rhythmic utterances, and movement explorations of early childhood, young children are primed and ready to create (Marsh & Young, 2006). Campbell and Scott-Kassner (2014) acknowledged this creative spark in young children, encouraging teachers to develop this natural tendency by facilitating opportunities for truly original thought, finding multiple ways to investigate the musical sounds they can make. This chapter brings young children into the realm of creative musicking using the world's musical cultures as a point of departure—in child-friendly ways, of course, including singing, dancing, using found sounds, and even playing instruments set up for children's maximal success.

As described and demonstrated in previous chapters, the World Music Pedagogy process features multiple dimensions and levels of depth of interaction with the world's musical cultures. Listening leads to young children's familiarity with the music, which leads to grasping parts and then the sum total of a musical selection in order for young children to be able to make the music their own. Beginning with the Attentive Listening stage, young children have the opportunity through multiple listenings to tune into the various elements of music in a purposeful way. Engaged Listening is a continuation of listening, again and again, getting so familiar with the music as to become active participants in it—singing a part of it, or playing a basic rhythm, or following in movement patterns that become easy over time, making music in some capacity while hearing the recorded or live sounds of the music under study. In Enactive Listening, the young children have aurally engaged with the music to the extent that they can launch performances of their world music excerpts. While this may seem like a culminating feature of the World Music Pedagogy process, it is really a springboard into the realm of composition and improvisation of children's own musical ideas. The continuum of Attentive Listening, Engaged Listening, and Enactive Listening are logical and foundational steps for young children to experience prior to delving into creative, original encounters. For the purposes of this discussion of young children's involvement in Creating World Music, composition refers to the creation of a musical entity in such a way that it will be performed repeatedly, and it may be notated by the teacher alone or with the children, using standard Western staff notation or other iconic means of graphically depicting the sound in ways that young children will understand. On the other hand, improvisation is used here to refer to on-the-spot musicking within a given musical context.

Frequently, the term "improvisation" conjures up the sophisticated music expression of a jazz pianist, or an Indian *sitar* player, or an Irish fiddler, or a Kenyan drummer, weaving musical tapestries while using complex tonal and/or rhythmic language. It is important to note that improvisation happens in many of the world's musical cultures and that it can develop through children's own capacities, at any age or level, given that the parameters are established appropriately. While a preschooler might not be able to perform a jazz solo, he can certainly improvise some vocal sounds or body percussion. The early childhood years are a training ground for motor skills, and young children can certainly use those movement impulses to improvise on small instruments or vocally. Instruments offer another important way for children to get their creative juices flowing, especially instruments that are adapted to small hands or can be altered in some way to accommodate the needs of early childhood. For example, a young child might be far more successful with a xylophone with only two or three bars rather than the whole spectrum of pitches offered or with a small hand drum rather than a large frame drum. Many of the pieces featured in this volume are programmatic in some way, allowing children a more concrete point of entry into understanding these musical cultures. Animals, weather, the seasons, nature, family, friends, and other narratives might inspire young children to spin their own tales inspired by the sounds they hear.

An easy doorway into the realm of improvisation is available through the Hawaiian hula mele "Anoai," one of the Learning Pathways that unify this volume. The lyrics of this mele tell of the rain hitting the petals of the lehua blossom, with the *'uli 'uli* gourd rattles (pictured in Chapter 2) providing not only the aural imagery of rain, but the rhythmic context for the chant. Listening in the previous stages is crucial, as young children can develop a concept of this Hawaiian aural sensibility and the imitation of nature through instrumental timbres. Using this concept as a springboard, young children may improvise new sounds that inspire thoughts and feelings of rain in Episode 5.1.

Episode 5.1: Lehua Blossoms in the Rain: Hawaiian Musical Storytelling (Learning Pathway #1)

(For Improvisation)

Specific Use: Ages 3 to 6

Materials:

- "Anoai," Jacob Feuerring with Tom Hiona, Smithsonian Folkways, classroom instruments as available (suggested: rain stick, shekere, glockenspiel, hand drums with small round plastic beads inside for making swirling sounds, cabasa, thunder tube)

Procedure:

1. "Music friends, you may remember our piece of music from Hawai'i that was about the rain and how it fell gently onto the lehua blossom petals. What did you hear that helped you think about rain?"
2. Field student answers (the sounds of the shakers, *'uli 'uli*).
3. "Let's try some different ways to make rain sounds to accompany 'Anoai.' You can make some rain sounds using body percussion! (Snap fingers gently, rub palms together, pat legs quickly, stomp feet for heavy rain.)
4. Play track and improvise body percussion rain sounds.
5. "We can also use some instruments to help us improvise the sounds we hear when it rains."
6. Model and distribute instruments, which might include rain sticks, shakers of various sizes and shapes, ocean drums or hand drums flipped over with small beads to roll around inside, or thunder tubes.
7. Play track and allow children to improvise with their instruments.

Composition and improvisation in the early childhood years might be as simple as creating a soundscape or sonic backdrop to accompany a piece of music, speech piece, or story. Young children might engage this form of creativity using the "Moli Hua" Learning Pathway excerpt in Episode 5.2 as a point of departure. The jasmine only emerges in its full form as night falls. Children can exercise their creativity in imagining what other sounds (either real or invented) might happen at night—crickets chirping, owls hooting, rain falling, frogs croaking, wind rustling leaves, stars twinkling, and so on. They may then assign timbres to these sounds using their voices, body percussion, classroom instruments, or sounds found in their immediate environment, such as tapping a pencil on a table. For example, stars twinkling might be represented by glockenspiel glissandos or crickets chirping might be represented by short cabasa rhythms. Children will need assistance in developing the appropriate vocabulary needed to describe instruments and timbres as well as assistance in how to notate and interpret their soundscape. By no means is the use of traditional Western music notation necessary—possible options include pictures of the instruments, photos of what the sounds are intended to represent, or simple lines or shapes that symbolize the sounds children wish to create. The progression of the World Music Pedagogy process, with its emphasis on listening, provides young children with myriad aural images to catapult them into their own explorations of sound.

Episode 5.2: The Gentle Jasmine: A Chinese Melody (Learning Pathway #2)

(For Creating)

Specific Use: Ages 3 to 6

Materials:

- "Moli Hua," Crystal Children's Choir & Karl Chang, iTunes, classroom instruments (child-selected), paper or whiteboard for documenting "notation" of soundscape

Procedure:

1. "Music friends, you have done a great job learning about the Chinese song 'Moli Hua' in lots of different kinds of ways. You remember that the jasmine only blooms at which time?"
2. Field student answers (nighttime).
3. "What are some other sounds you hear at nighttime?"
4. Field student answers (will vary—may include insects, wind, rain, traffic, or even imagined sounds). Make a list on the board.
5. "Let's decide what kind of instrument sounds or voice sounds or body percussion sounds could match these ideas. Let's also decide on a way we can show that sound with a picture."
6. Discuss.
7. "Let's decide which one of these should go first, second, and so on."
8. Determine an order.
9. "All right, music friends! We are ready to play our nighttime composition along with our piece, 'Moli Hua.'"
10. Play track. Play notated soundscape. Repeat/adjust as desired.

As noted previously, composition and improvisation may bring to mind skilled adult musicians, the Indian sitarist, or the stoic symphonic composer bent over a sheet of candlelit staff paper pouring forth his newest masterpiece. While these are certainly important threads in the tapestry of musical creativity, they are not the only options. Musical creativity takes on different meanings and manifestations in different cultural contexts and must do so, as well, in the early childhood years, as developmental characteristics are considered. Challenges to these creative endeavors might be present in the motor skills of the children of this age and stage. For example, a florid saxophone solo might be out of the question, but an improvisation of claps and stomps is entirely within the realm of possibility. Another challenge might be the issue of purposeful improvisation as opposed to making noise—young children can be exceedingly good at both. The following "Tera Xylophone" encounter in Episode 5.3 helps little ones grasp the meaning of improvisation, using the world music selection as a point of departure, rather than seeking out an opportunity to make noise!

Episode 5.3: X Marks the Spot: Xylophones of West Africa (Learning Pathway #3)

(For Improvisation)

Specific Use: Ages 5 to 7

Materials:

- "Tera Xylophone," Music from the Villages of Northeastern Nigeria, Smithsonian Folkways, Boomwhackers (Ab, Db, Eb), tone bells (Db, Eb, F, Ab, Bb), photograph of West African xylophone

Procedures:

1. "Listen to my piece of music and raise your hand when you remember the name of this musical instrument and where in the world it comes from."
2. Play track.
3. Field student answers (xylophone, Nigeria, Africa).
4. "In some musical cultures in the world, people might make up what they are playing on the spot. That might sound funny, but it has a fancy name called 'improvisation.' That does not mean you make up things that are silly or that do not fit with the music. It means that you use the music as a guide to make up your own things that go with the music. You can have a chance to improvise, too, using the tone bells and Boomwhackers. Try to make your improvisation fit with the music—you can match how soft or loud, how fast or slow, or how choppy or smooth the music is."
5. Distribute instruments.
6. Play track. Children improvise.
7. Repeat as desired.

While young children are capable of great things, it may be best to start out simply when diving into composition and improvisation. The following episode featuring the Caribbean steelpan tune "Coqui" does just that by inviting children to improvise using what they already have—their voices and the space around them. The Spanish term "coqui" translates to frog, setting the stage for vocal exploration using animal sounds as a point of departure. When the door is opened to experimenting with sound, children will surely have no difficulty in finding something to offer. World Music Pedagogy calls upon teachers to facilitate improvisation and composition experiences that reflect the stylistic attributes demonstrated by the selected recordings or live musicking models. Again, the age and stage of early childhood must be considered—while these blossoming musicians may not yet be able to manipulate a steelpan ensemble, they can certainly play off the amphibious programmatic spirit of "Coqui."

Born in the Caribbean islands, the steelpan is an instrument that speaks to the heart of improvisation and ingenuity. Having been taken away from their homes, slaves brought their musical expressions to the islands from western African cultures and nations. In Trinidad, as elsewhere in the Caribbean, the African diaspora enriched the music of this region, bringing with it rhythmic sophistication, in layers upon layers of syncopation, that inspires lively dancing at home, in dance halls, in community centers, in churches, and on the street. Trinidadians of African origin used the oil drums that washed up on the shores of the Caribbean beaches to craft musical instruments along with any other materials they could access. The resulting unique sound of rhythms, melodies, and harmonies has become synonymous with the Caribbean region of the world. Modern steelpans involve a layer of metal stretched over a large cylindrical container. The metallic overlay is then hammered into ovals with corresponding pitches. Children quickly latch on to the concept that the larger ovals produce lower sounds and vice versa.

The Invaders, the ensemble heard in the following recording, are founding fathers of sorts of steelpan music, having passed on the traditions of crafting and playing these ingenious instruments to generations of Trinidadians. Episode 5.4 first invites children to listen for the ascending interval featured in the higher pitched steelpan that is representative of the "ribbit" sound they may associate with frogs. Next, young children are given the opportunity to improvise with what they have around them—just like The Invaders and other ingenious steelpan pioneers!

Episode 5.4: Froggy Friends From the Caribbean Islands

(For Improvisation)

Specific Use: Ages 3 to 6

Materials:

- "Coqui," The Invaders, Smithsonian Folkways

Procedure:

1. "Listen to my piece of music. You will hear a higher pitched steelpan making a sound that goes from low to high. Try to figure out which animal sound the instrument is trying to sound like."

2. Play track.
3. Field student answers.
4. "If you were thinking a frog, then you have the right answer! This song is called 'Coqui,' which means frog in Spanish. It is played by instruments called steelpans that come from the Caribbean islands. Let's listen again and raise your hand when you think you hear the steelpans play a ribbit sound."
5. Play track.
6. "Great job! This time when you hear the ribbit sound, use your voice to make the best frog sound you can!"
7. Play track.
8. "Here is a challenge for you. A neat thing about steelpans is that they were made from giant metal containers that washed up on the beach. People found these containers and started tapping them, making musical sounds. Like the people of steelpan cultures, we can also use the things around us to make sounds, too. Listen, and when you hear the ribbit sound, you can make your own ribbit sound using your hands, feet, fingers, voice, floor, walls, anything around you! You might choose to clap, snap, stomp, tap on the floor!"
9. Play track.

A more challenging improvisatory endeavor may come in the form of an upbeat Tahitian pop tune. Study of the world's musical cultures frequently conjures up images of delving into the traditional, the long-lasting, the foundational sounds that have been produced by cultures over extensive periods of time. However, it is important to recall that musical cultures are still proliferating, the traditional and the contemporary coming together in ways that are meaningful for modern generations. "Tutuki" by the contemporary pop group known as Te Vaka gives young children a taste of the still-continuing musical flavors of the Pacific Islands, such as the sounds of the log drums and traditional languages indigenous to this region of the world. Episode 5.5 invites the use of barred percussion instruments with various pitches selectively removed (Figure 5.2), young children are free to improvise along with the buoyant beats of "Tutuki" (Figure 5.3).

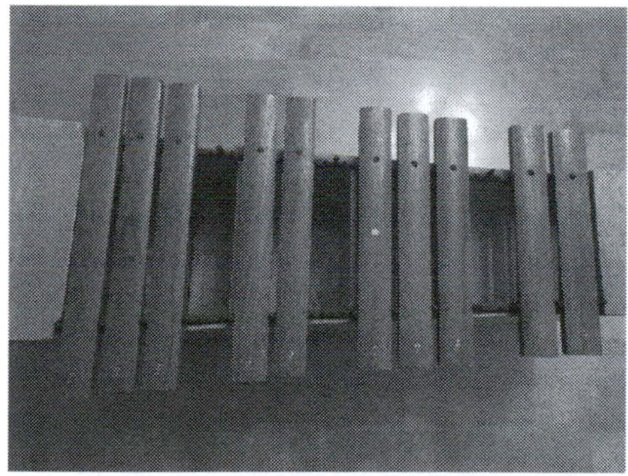

Figure 5.2 Orff xylophone with bars set to C pentatonic scale for "*Tutuki*"

Figure 5.3 Four-year-old jamming on the xylophone

Episode 5.5: Proud Tahitian Tunes

(For Improvisation)

Specific Use: Pre-K through Kindergarten

Materials:

- "Tutuki," Te Vaka, iTunes, Orff xylophones (set to the C pentatonic scale), mallets, scarves or ribbons for movement

Procedure:

1. "Listen to my piece of music and tell me if this is exciting music for dancing or a lullaby for going to sleep."
2. Play track.
3. Field student answers (music for dancing!).
4. "Yes! Our piece of music is for dancing! This song called 'Tutuki' comes from an island called Tahiti. The song is all about feeling the beat and being proud of our music and dancing. I will hand you a scarf (or ribbon or other movement manipulative), and you may use it to show me how the music sounds to you."
5. Distribute scarves.

6. Play track.
7. "Let's add something creative and special to our piece of music that we can also be proud of. You may dance with your scarf, but when I give you a signal, you may come and play the xylophone along with Te Vaka. You may use your mallets to play any bars you like! When your turn is over, you may go back to dancing."
8. Play track.
9. Cycle through the dancers. Consider the use of multiple xylophones to facilitate everyone having a turn.

The previous episodes engage children in improvisation through instrument play, found sounds, and body percussion, but Episode 5.6 brings children's voices into the mix with some vocal jazz. Scat singing is a phenomenon commonly found in American jazz, using vocables or nonsense syllables to make music. If there is one thing at which young children can excel, it is making nonsensical yet musical vocal sounds! The jazz standard "It Don't Mean a Thing (If It Ain't Got That Swing)" gets children swinging with the cool sounds of the Duke Ellington Orchestra. Throughout the World Music Pedagogy process, young children are introduced to diversity in music and people; as such, Duke Ellington provides a compelling case study of a phenomenal model of musicianship and innovation. Originally from the Washington, D.C., area, Duke Ellington was a skilled pianist, composer, and ensemble leader whose originality forever left a mark on the landscape of American music. Children will love the "doo-wah" scat syllables in this episode and will undoubtedly be excited to create some of their own!

Episode 5.6: It Don't Mean a Thing: Scatting With the Duke

(For Improvisation)

Specific Use: Ages 5 to 7

Materials:

- "It Don't Mean a Thing (If It Ain't Got That Swing)," Duke Ellington Orchestra, iTunes

Procedure:

1. "Music friends, please listen to my piece of music and raise your hand when you hear some words that might be silly made-up words."
2. Play track. Assess hand raising on "doo-wah" syllables.

3. "Looks like you heard some silly words! What were they?"
4. Field answers.
5. "These nonsense words are actually an important part of this kind of music called jazz. We call it 'scat singing' when a singer uses these kinds of pretend words to sing. Let's listen again and join in singing when we hear the 'doo-wah' scat words."
6. Play track. Sing along.
7. "There are all kinds of words we can use for scatting, like 'ba,' 'doo,' 'bee,' 'shoo,' and anything else you can imagine. I bet that all of you can make up some scat words, too. Let's listen to our song again, and when we hear the scat words, you can sing your own inventions!"
8. Play track. Children scat.

Improvisation of movement offers yet another way for children to engage with music in a spontaneous yet guided way. To culminate the improvisation episodes is an encounter with the work of English composer Edward Elgar. Elgar began composing during his childhood years, bringing his imaginary worlds to life through music. In his orchestral work "The Wand of Youth," Elgar features a movement entitled "Fairies and Giants" which has long been popular in exchanges with young children as a listening excerpt and inspiration for movement. Episode 5.7 invites children to improvise movements that match the higher-pitched melodies of the fairies and the low-pitched strains of the giants.

Episode 5.7: Moving High and Low

(For Improvisation)

Specific Use: Ages 4 to 7

Materials:

- "Fairies and Giants from The Wand of Youth Suite," Sir Edward Elgar and the London Symphony Orchestra, iTunes

Procedure:

1. "Let's listen to my piece of music, and please raise your hand when you hear instruments playing high sounds."
2. Play track. Assess listening.
3. "Good work! Let's listen again, and raise your hand when you hear low sounds."

4. Play track. Assess listening.
5. "This piece of music was composed by a man named Edward Elgar. He had a very good imagination, just like all of you. He imagined that the high parts of this piece sounded like fairies and the low parts of this piece sounded like giants. Do you think he made good choices for which characters match which kind of music?"
6. Field answers.
7. "Your next job is to listen carefully to the music, and you may improvise a dance to go with the high parts of the music and the low parts of the music. What could a dance look like that matches with the high music?"
8. Field answers.
9. "What could a dance look like that matches with the low music?"
10. Field answers.
11. "Let's give it a try! Find your own space on the floor, and you may create different dances for the high and low parts of the music."
12. Play track and dance.

Exploring the East African instrument, the *mbira*, is a delight for all ages, especially young children. Its timbre is almost otherworldly, with the undulating rhythms and melodies streaming from just simple arrangements of metal and wood. Developed centuries ago in various regions of Africa, such as Zimbabwe, the *mbira* is somewhat improvisatory in and of itself—*mbiras* have been crafted using what is available to the instrument maker. *Mbiras* frequently feature bottlecaps from glass bottles that are intended to provide a nice vibrating buzz as the metal tines are engaged. It is not uncommon to see one's favorite soda brand represented on a musical instrument. *Mbiras* have even been made using what would seemingly be trash—even olive oil cans have found new life as *mbiras*! Episode 5.8 capitalizes upon the wonder that *mbiras* inspire through the creation and playing of a homemade *mbira*.

Episode 5.8: The 'Mazing *Mbira*

(For Creating)

Specific Use: Ages 4 to 7

Materials:

- "Taireva," The Soul of Mbira: Traditions of the Shona People, iTunes, *mbira* or photograph of *mbira*, craft sticks, binder clips, markers

Procedure:

1. "Listen to my piece of music and try to figure out how many different kinds of instruments you hear. Hold up the number on your fingers when you think you have it figured out!"
2. Play track.
3. Field student answers (just one kind of instrument—*mbira*).
4. "That might have been a tricky thing to figure out—what kinds of sounds did you hear that might have made you think it was more than one instrument?"
5. Field answers (rattling sound, melodic sound).
6. "This is a very special instrument from East Africa called a *mbira.* A group of people called the Shona people enjoy creating these instruments and playing beautiful music with them. Sometimes they use the things around them, even things that people threw away, to make their instruments, like cans and bottlecaps! Let's use things we have in our classroom to make our own *mbiras*."
7. Assist children in the crafting of their *mbiras* with craft sticks and binder clips. They may decorate with markers if desired.
8. Invite children to play a steady beat on their *mbiras* along with the recording.
9. Play track.
10. Invite children to play a rhythm of their own creation.
11. Play track.

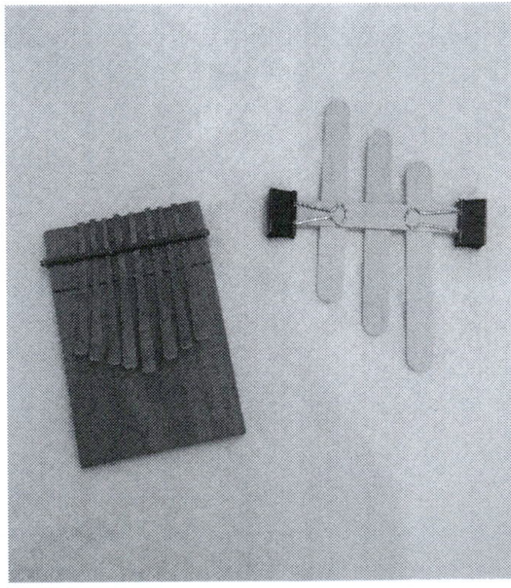

Figure 5.4 *Mbiras*, authentic and homemade

As young children demonstrate the emergent skill of keeping a steady beat, they may be ready for something a bit more challenging in the realm of rhythmic performance. Episode 5.9 featuring "Oye Como Va" might just be the remedy for young children ready for a next step. This beloved Latin jazz tune features the cha cha cha rhythm and invites children to begin feeling the groove with a furry feline friend, the Cha Cha Cha Kitty (Figure 5.5). As children listen, they "pet" the kitty in a rhythmic fashion, making this ubiquitous rhythm accessible and concrete. Once they have the groove down, they may experiment with timbres, trying out the cha cha cha pattern on different instruments (Figure 5.6) or even creating cha cha cha versions of their favorite nursery rhymes or folk songs. This recording features the musical stylings of Tito Puente, long known as a staple among Latin jazz artists. His fusions of Puerto Rican inspirations and American jazz inspire children and adults alike to get up and dance!

Episode 5.9: Hey! How's It Going?

(For Creating)

Specific Use: Ages 4 to 7

Materials:

- "Oye Como Va," Tito Puente, iTunes, Cha Cha Cha Kitty Listening Map (one for each child), various classroom instruments (suggested: guiro, shakers, rhythm sticks)

Procedure:

1. "Listen to my piece of music and move however the music makes you feel!"
2. Play track.
3. "This piece is called 'Oye Come Va.' This music has sounds that come from a place called Puerto Rico, and it is often used for dancing. There is a special rhythm in this music that goes 'cha cha cha—cha cha cha.' Let's listen and put that rhythm in our bodies."
4. Play track. Put cha cha cha (ta titi ta titi) rhythm in hands, feet, etc.
5. Here is a little friend who will help us feel that special cha cha cha rhythm—the Cha Cha Cha Kitty! After I give you your own kitty, you will get to pet him on the spots on the paper to help you feel the rhythm.
6. Play track.
7. "Thanks, Cha Cha Cha Kitty! Let's put that rhythm on some instruments! We usually hear this instrument called the guiro play that rhythm. It is an instrument that we hold with one hand and use a stick in the other hand to scrape across the top to play the cha cha cha rhythm. Even if we do not have a guiro, we can try our pattern on some other instruments, too.

8. Distribute instruments.
9. Play track. Play cha cha cha rhythm along to "Oye Como Va."
10. Extend the activity by playing the cha cha cha rhythm over other songs of the children's choosing to create new versions of familiar favorites.

Figure 5.5 Cha Cha Cha Kitty listening map/tapping page

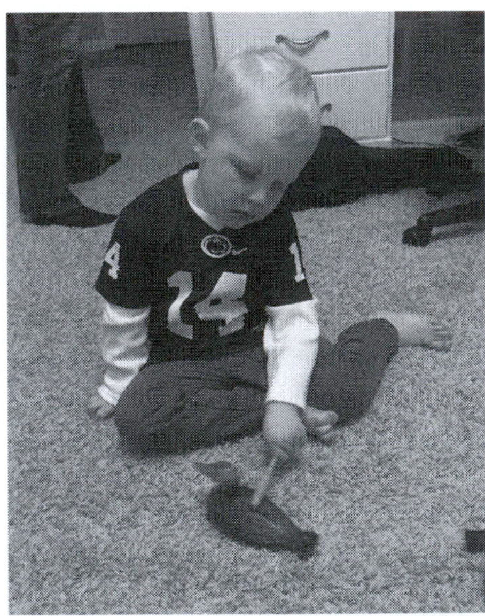

Figure 5.6 Toddler with a duck-shaped guiro

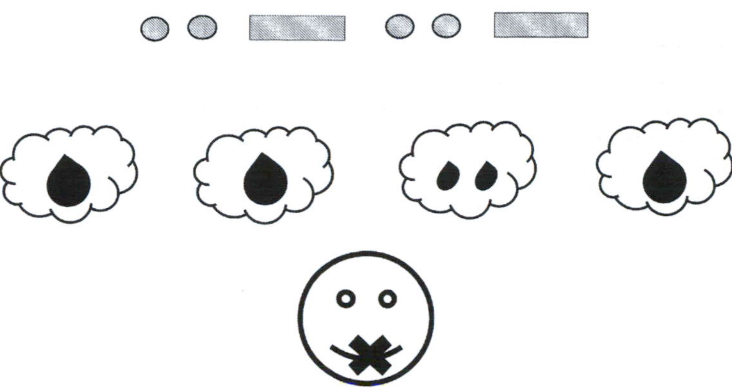

Figure 5.7 Examples of iconic notation for early childhood music

Notation further complicates the issue of composition as many young children have not yet learned to read their native languages, let alone a form of music notation, Western or otherwise. The creative and resourceful teacher knows her learners and uses a variety of approaches or iconic notation procedures to help children create and re-create their own musical ideas. See Figure 5.7 for various possibilities.

The following episode presents children and teachers with the opportunity to explore composition and notation in the context of a game. The children and teachers learn to play the counting out game from Ghana "Si Si Si," in which feet are tapped to a steady beat. This game was collected many decades ago by ethnomusicologists, who observed 3- to 6-year-old children playing it. In this game, whoever is tapped last is out! Where these kinds of games become challenging is how to engage the students who have gotten "out." In Episode 5.10, getting "out" is a reward, an opportunity to play an accompanying instrument. The teacher and children collaboratively decide which rhythms to compose and how to notate them on visuals that match the shape of the instruments the children will play.

Episode 5.10: Games From Ghana: Who's Out?

(For Creating)

Specific Use: Ages 5 to 6

Materials:

- "Si Si Si," Kojo Fosu & Edwina Hunter, Smithsonian Folkways Recordings, classroom instruments (suggested: hand drums, triangles, shakers), and circle-, triangle-, and egg-shaped paper visuals for displaying rhythms

Procedure:

1. "Listen to my piece of music and tap your toes to the beat."
2. Play track.
3. "Let's listen again and tap your neighbor's toes!"
4. Play track.
5. "Sometimes songs are meant to be enjoyed as games! This game is called Si Si Si and is played by children in the West African country called Ghana. Let's play the game! First, we need to make a circle. I will choose a leader. When the music plays, the leader will tap each person's feet in order down the line. If the leader taps your foot on the last word of the song, you will pull that foot back out of the circle and only have one foot in the game. If you get two feet out, you will scoot back out of the circle. Let's try."
6. Teacher appoints a leader.
7. Play track.
8. "If you are 'out' in this game, you are going to have a special job to do. You will go to an instrument station and play along with the rest of the friends playing the game. The sign shaped like a triangle shows what the triangles will play. The sign shaped like a circle shows what the hand drums will play. The sign shaped like an egg shows what the shakers will play. Let's work together to decide what rhythm each group will play.
9. Invite children to make suggestions of what rhythms to play and how to notate on the visuals.
10. Play track as needed for several children to have turns playing the game and playing instruments. Assist as needed.

One of the challenges for teachers of early childhood music is simply carving out the time and space for creative explorations of composition and improvisation to unfold. The following story highlights a little one who took command of her musical environment and decided to explore on her own.

The preschool music class of 3-, 4-, and 5-year-olds is about to conclude. The morning's excitement is winding down with a goodbye song, the same one sung each week to signal the end of the music session and alert the children that a transition back to their classroom is imminent. While most children are cheerful and engaged, Maria is having a rough morning. Tears, shouts, and general fussiness characterized her participation this morning. But despite her challenges, she is still compelled to make music—on her terms. She scoots over to the teacher's right side. The teacher has her guitar ready for the goodbye song, a purple plastic guitar pick in her right hand. Maria very gently touches the guitar strings—exploratory and experimental. She next takes the teacher's right hand in her own, moving the teacher's hand up and down on the strings. Top to bottom, top to bottom. By this time a hush has befallen the room, enveloping all teachers, caregivers, student interns, and children.

Maria is "doing music!" Maria then takes the teacher's hand and moves up and down on the strings in the syncopated strumming pattern the teacher frequently uses. In this moment, Maria is in control of the music, creating what she wants to create, using the teacher and the guitar as a scaffold. Perhaps the morning's other activities did not engage her, but the guitar certainly captured her imagination; perhaps she was inspired by the strains of Spanish guitar that accompanied the morning's free movement. It was clear she had studied both the recorded selection and the teacher's live model very closely in order to be able to manipulate the teacher's hand as she did. The teacher watches intently, waiting to see what will unfold.

Composition and improvisation are not necessarily neat, tidy processes—not for adults, not for children. Many teachers may enter their teaching life with fears and anxieties about their creative capacities in these areas. One of the most important things teachers and caregivers can do for their children's musical creativity is to accept, embrace, and exercise their own. Early childhood musical creativity can get messy, but while this process might not be the easiest to facilitate, it is certainly worthwhile. As in the vignette prior, sometimes little ones just need some space, time, and support to try things out.

Teacher Feature: Mrs. Jocelyn Manzanarez

Jocelyn Manzanarez of Musically Minded, Inc.

In Mrs. Jocelyn Manzanarez's musical world it is "all about doing," and she is intent upon stimulating little ones to experience musical cultures near and far in their everyday lives. Mrs. Manzanarez is the owner of Musically Minded, Inc., a Seattle-based early childhood music company. This company sends dynamic music educators out into early childhood learning centers, preschools, and daycares to facilitate 30-minute weekly music classes for children ages birth through 5 years old. Mrs. Manzanarez describes these hands-on music classes as an "exploratory experience where we want children to realize they are all musicians and born with the ability to create music." These exciting musical encounters provide early childhood music learners with a wide range of experiences, including movement, singing, playing instruments, storytelling, and listening to a variety of musical sounds. World Music Pedagogy makes careful and purposeful use of musical listening and builds upon the listening in order to offer opportunities to express music creatively through the use of elemental features derived from the music that young children have experienced by ear. One might be challenged by the possibility of engaging children from birth through pre-Kindergarten in any type of meaningful musical listening or creating experience. Mrs. Manzanarez has accepted this challenge, embracing the essential nature of cultivating musical facility in early childhood.

Q: In the process of World Music Pedagogy, we move from Attentive Listening into the more hands-on stages of Engaged Listening and Enactive Listening. Where it can get tricky is the creating and performing aspect. I don't want to underestimate what little kids can do, but I also want to think about what is appropriate for the brain and body developmentally during early childhood. Can you speak to some of the ways you have little ones perform and create using music of the world's cultures as a springboard?
A: It's so tough because I feel like we have such a short amount of time with them. I wonder if it would be different if I was with them all day long and we had more time to work on things. We might have children listen to a recorded track and have them play a steady beat, or just play as they wish. Or see how the music makes them move in an improvisatory way.

Q: Sometimes it can be challenging to navigate the line of formality in instruction with early childhood, wanting to go deeper but keeping things appropriate for the age level.
A: Yes. How do we move away from the teacher-directed "now do this, now do this" model to allowing kids to be more free. There's no right answer. It's just "do" for the sake of "doing."

Q: Can you speak further to your business and how that is an effective vehicle for getting music into the lives of little ones.
A: Yes. Being in a childcare center, we can provide music classes for working families. And I believe that's important because parents are super busy. We want them to be with their child, yes, that would be awesome, but the fact is that doesn't always happen. If we don't provide these classes then kids might not get it at all because it would have to happen on the weekends or at night and that can be a busy time. By doing that we are able to get kids that are already there and enhance their day.

Q: Would you describe your philosophy of incorporating music listening into early childhood music instruction?
A: I love to incorporate listening! The way that I feel about it is that it actually allows children to stop and be calm, yet have a focus. In our world we have so much going. So many advertisements, so many people talking and vying for our attention. It happens with kids as well. By [listening to music] I do believe that it allows them to work that

muscle of self-control and focus. When we do purposeful listening activities, I've seen how it affects children. It happens too often for it to just be a coincidence. What happens is the kids literally focus. They pay attention. I can get the child who is usually off-task to tune in. That interests me. Why is that happening? Why are they so keyed into what you might think would be the opposite? Something so specific that they wouldn't be able to focus, but instead, it has this consistent response. They're all ears. I always pair [listening] with a visual. That's something that I've found to be really important. You want to tap into at least two of the senses. Whenever I'm working with teachers, I'm always talking about that. "Do you have at least two senses being awakened?" The brain seems to want to stay with something as long as they're not bored, and really, by having that extra stimulation, you can keep them pretty focused.

Q: What kinds of visuals do you use for listening encounters?
A: Could be felt [pieces for the felt board]. I want kids to know what [instruments] actually look like. An actual picture of a French horn or a picture of a bird. The other thing that I've used which has been a huge hit is the real deal! I do a song called "Sounds in the House." I brought in a doll house! In the doll house I had a baby and the dog and the cat [to make the sounds.] They've seen things like that before, so there's familiarity. It's amazing the focus they demonstrate!

Q: I'm curious about the infants. A lot of people are surprised to learn that infant and toddler music classes exist. Can you speak to how you facilitate listening with the tiny ones?
A: Same thing! I love doing [listening activities] with the infants—they can't figure out where [the sound] is coming from! They can't find that sound source. Watching them look around, paying attention, "What is that? Where is it coming from?" I still do this with them. With the toddlers, same thing. They are not verbally talking back to me about what they think about [the music they are hearing], but I can see that they are responding to it. They know it, they recognize it, they know something is different.

Q: If they are looking for the sound source, it seems as though they are working on the important developmental milestone of tracking sounds.
A: Exactly.

Q: If you were to give advice to teachers who would like to incorporate listening effectively into the early childhood setting, what would you suggest?
A: Make sure that kids are involved in "doing" it. It's not a performance situation where the teacher plays the guitar and the kids are expected to sit and listen. That's not developmentally appropriate. A teacher was saying the other day, "I was trying to explain the instrument before passing it out and this toddler was wanting to reach and grab the instrument." Yes. Because they want to be involved! Make sure you have activities that kids are totally involved in. They don't want this to be a spectator sport.

Cultivating Creativity

Creativity and improvisation are part of the daily landscape of human life. Moving from one place to another, crafting conversations with others, these seemingly mundane tasks are living proof of the presence and necessity of the creative act. Inviting these creative impulses into the realm of early childhood music simply extends these impulses, shaping thought and sound and movement into something new and unique. Children in their early childhood years are not too young to experience the autonomy and agency of musical creativity and improvisation.

References

Campbell, P. S. & Scott-Kassner, C. (2014). *Music in childhood* (4th Ed.). Belmont, CA: Thomson.

Marsh, K. & Young, S. (2006). Musical play. In G. E. McPherson (Ed.), *The child as musician: A handbook of musical development*. New York, NY: Oxford University Press.

Listening Episodes—Learning Pathways

"Anoai," Jacob Feuerring with Tom Hiona, Smithsonian Folkways, *hula kahiko* featuring *'uli 'uli* gourd rattles www.folkways.si.edu/hawaiian-dancers-male-singer/anoai-hula-uliuli/hawaii/music/track/smithsonian

"Moli Hua," Crystal Children's Choir & Karl Chang, iTunes, choral arrangement of traditional Chinese melody https://itunes.apple.com/WebObjects/MZStore.woa/wa/viewCollaboration?cc=us&ids=431607970-431607973

"Tera Xylophone," Music from the Villages of Northeastern Nigeria, Smithsonian Folkways, traditional xylophones of West Africa www.folkways.si.edu/music-of-the-tera-people-tera-xylophone-music/world/music/track/smithsonian

Listening Episodes

"Coqui," The Invaders, Smithsonian Folkways, programmatic steelpan piece about a frog www.folkways.si.edu/the-invaders/coqui/caribbean-world/music/track/smithsonian

"Tutuki," Te Vaka, iTunes, Tahitian popular music https://itunes.apple.com/us/album/tutuki/id294146772?i=294146840

"It Don't Mean a Thing (If It Ain't Got That Swing)," Duke Ellington Orchestra, iTunes, jazz standard featuring scat singing https://itunes.apple.com/us/album/it-dont-mean-a-thing-if-it-aint-got-that-swing/879566951?i=879567004

"Fairies and Giants from The Wand of Youth Suite," Sir Edward Elgar and the London Symphony Orchestra, iTunes, orchestral piece featuring high- and low-pitched melodies https://itunes.apple.com/us/album/the-wand-of-youth-suite-no-1-op-1a-vii-fairies-and-giants/422506122?i=422506129

"Taireva," The Soul of Mbira: Traditions of the Shona People, iTunes, East African *mbira* music https://itunes.apple.com/us/album/taireva/id300988636?i=300988724

"Oye Como Va," Tito Puente, iTunes, Latin jazz piece featuring the cha cha cha rhythm https://itunes.apple.com/us/album/oye-como-va/id79674516?i=79674566

"Si Si Si," Kojo Fosu & Edwina Hunter, Smithsonian Folkways, African children's counting out game www.folkways.si.edu/kojo-fosu-and-edwina-hunter/si-si-si/childrens/music/track/smithsonian

6

Integrating World Music

Miss Davidson unloaded the colorful, musical contents of her car into a rolling cart, slung her guitar case onto her back, and headed into the daycare center. Upon entering the preschool classroom, delighted shouts of "music!" filled the air, followed by little ones scurrying to their circle time spots as fast as their tiny feet could carry them. A new unit was to begin in preschool music class that day, something new and different that the children, all 3 to 4 years of age, would find fun and compelling. After the compulsory hello song, Miss Davidson extracted a bright and colorful book from her cart and began chanting rhythmically:

> *Around the world we go,*
> *to learn what we don't know.*
> *In foreign lands, we'll all shake hands,*
> *As around the world we go!*
> *Around the world we go,*
> *In singing we can show*
> *A way to play in a friendly way,*
> *As around the world we go!*
>
> (*Brown, 2012*)

This excerpt from the story Around the World We Go *by Margaret Wise Brown represents a child-friendly way to enter into the study of and participation in the world's musical expressions. The teacher reveals an oversized passport prop and displays it to the children, signaling something special that is about to begin! A symbol of world travel, adventure, and exploration, the passport becomes a unifying agent in this fun and friendly journey through various musical cultures of the world. The young children were permitted to enter the flags of all the places they visited throughout their unit into the giant passport. Encompassing singing, rhythmic chanting and vocalizations, movement, listening, improvisation, composition, instrumental performance, storytelling, manipulatives, and even thoughtful discussion, the world music unit had begun.*

Over the course of the next several weeks, the 3- and 4-year-olds found themselves not only "visiting" many new lands through their musicking but also contextualizing, synthesizing, and making connections to other aspects of their lives. In their study of the musical expressions of China, they chanted poetry, sang songs, and played a "drop the handkerchief" game. They studied a papier-mâché dragon head used for Lunar New Year parades as well as a marionette of a Chinese dragon and the features of the many animals that it comprises, such as scales of a fish and claws of an eagle. A musical trip to the Andes mountains of South America found the preschoolers singing, playing games, performing folk dances, and exploring the exciting world of traditional flutes of Ecuador, Peru, Bolivia, and the northern regions of Chile and Argentina. In studying the siku (panpipe), the children discussed the physics of sound by answering questions about which part of the siku makes the low sounds and which part makes the high sounds. Thus, acoustical connections were made, with children understanding that the longer the tube, the lower the pitch of the sound it produces.

A brief visit to Spain invited preschoolers to sample the sounds of the flamenco with vigorous strums of the guitar. They even tried out some child-friendly castanets, small, plastic, and joined with a band on one side to facilitate opening and closing. A handmade fan from Madrid was passed around, demonstrating that functional objects in Spain and elsewhere are often crafted and painted to be small works of art, too. Visiting Hawai'i was exciting as well, with students singing and performing a hula noho, or a seated hula using only the hands to tell the story. They sang of a singing snail, an endangered species, a designation they were quick to report means that there are few of these snails left. They further explored the culture of Hawai'i with a musical storytelling of how the taro plant, a starchy root vegetable and staple food of the traditional Hawaiians, is cultivated. Through this story, the young children learned of the native Hawaiians' reverence for the earth and the dedication it takes to preserve the precious resources of the land. Young children are often surprised to learn that Hawai'i was at one time its very own kingdom with its own language, music, instruments, and stories and legends.

Traveling to East Africa to play some children's games was a highlight of the preschoolers' world music unit. They learned to play a Tanzanian game with the Swahili words for stand up, sit down, and jump! The young children were intrigued to discover that the Tanzanian children who learn these Swahili words at school might speak an entirely different indigenous language in their homes with their families. It was an exceptional treat to play and to explore tempo (it is fun when it is fast!), but more importantly, this playful tune showed the preschool children that kids all over the world enjoy musical games. The unit culminated with so much more than music being made—children explored culture, lifeways, and important traditions of other lands. Their exploration also intersected with mythology, cultural celebrations, the physics of sound, visual arts, ecology, language, and social customs of the world's children. This cross-curricular integration is a valuable component to the practice of World Music Pedagogy in an early childhood setting.

Bringing It All Together: Integration

The integration of World Music Pedagogy with other content areas is a next logical step in this process of listening to learn about the world's musical cultures. Children have much to say and share about what they hear and know and enjoy making connections to other aspects of their lives. Music is something that cannot be compartmentalized—it is not only something to be engaged with during a weekly music class led by a music teacher. Rather, music touches all aspects of human life. It is a part of the rituals and celebrations of the world's people, everything from feast days and festivals, to the ubiquitous "Happy Birthday" songs sung to celebrate an individual. Music belongs to people, belongs in contexts, belongs in time, making this an important aspect of young children's foundational musical experiences. There are many points of departure available for integrating music with other content areas with young children, beginning with careful listening of the world's musical cultures. This chapter aspires to assist teachers in recognizing the many and varied connections between music and content areas typically addressed in early childhood programs such as Language Arts, Science, Visual Arts, Mathematics, Physical Education, and Social Studies. Each content area is introduced with an overview and is followed by episodes to help bring these important musical integrations to life for young children. The Learning Pathway selections are used again in this chapter, bringing young children's careful listening and active musicking to an even higher level of meaning and relevance through integration.

Language Arts

Children are natural storytellers and often demonstrate a command of language and communication that seems well beyond their years. Their work in the Language Arts arena is multifaceted in order to prepare them for a lifetime of effective exchanges with others. Children learn book skills, that is, how to appropriately treat books, turn pages in the correct order, and identify authors and illustrators. They work through the nuts and bolts of language, dealing with the syllables and sounds and phonemes that appear in words. They construct simple sentences to express thoughts and share stories, either retelling familiar stories or communicating stories of their own creation. Comprehension and recall of text are addressed as well, inviting children to answer questions about things they have just heard or read.

Storytelling is a compelling aspect of human life—consider the many television programs, films, stage plays, novels, documentaries, and art forms that humans have constructed, adapted, manipulated, and implemented just for the sake of telling a story. Young children are no different! The act of storytelling is just as compelling for little ones, too. The Learning Pathway feature in Episode 6.1, "Anoai," represents one of the most beautiful storytelling forms, the hula. In ages past when the Hawaiian language was not written down, hula served a very important purpose in the preservation and transmission of stories. Extending in to contemporary times, Hawaiians engage in the act of "talk story," a term that encompasses catching up with friends and connecting socially. "Anoai" might present young children with an opportunity to challenge their narrative spinning skills. Further engagement in both storytelling and Hawaiian culture may be found in the children's book *Old Makana Had a Taro Farm*. Similar to his rural continental American counterpart, Old MacDonald, the main character, Old Makana, has a farm full of animals and even takes children through the process of cultivating taro (including eating it at a lu'au). The Barefoot Natives' soundtrack to the story is sure to delight teachers and children alike as they sing along and even learn the Hawaiian vocabulary terms for the various animals Old Makana has on his farm.

Episode 6.1: Lehua Blossoms in the Rain: Hawaiian Musical Storytelling (Learning Pathway #1)

(For Integrating)

Specific Use: Ages 3 to 6

Materials:

- "Anoai," Jacob Feuerring with Tom Hiona, Smithsonian Folkways, art supplies such as crayons, markers, paints, etc.

Procedure:

1. "One of the very special things about Hawaiian hula meles is that they are ways to tell stories using words, instruments, and dance. What are some other ways to tell stories?"
2. Discuss answers (movies, books, comic strips, etc.).
3. "Let's use our Hawaiian piece as a story starter. 'The rain fell onto the lehua blossoms and then . . .'"
4. Children complete the story prompt with their own ideas. While the possibilities are endless, children may also be prompted to work within some of the cultural matters of Hawaiian sensibility, such as reverence of the land or loyalty to family.
5. Invite children to illustrate their stories and use their artwork as a scaffold in retelling their stories.

Consider the exquisite art form of Balinese shadow puppetry. Fusing storytelling, drama, music, and visual arts, Indonesian shadow puppetry can be a compelling point of entry for young children to explore the many connections between Language Arts and musical cultures of the world. Although *wayang* may refer to a performance involving the movement of shadow puppets or real live people, the aspect of puppetry seems particularly appealing to young children, as well as a more accessible format to teachers across the globe. Episode 6.2 calls upon teachers and children to integrate their listening with storytelling, using the Indonesian *wayang* as a point of departure.

Episode 6.2: Me and My Shadow: Telling Stories Through Balinese Shadow Puppetry

(For Integrating)

Specific Use: Ages 5 to 7

Materials:

- "Wayang Sasak: Rangsang," Sekaha Sekar Karya, Smithsonian Folkways, video clip of *wayang*, map of the world, black construction paper, tape, popsicle sticks, white sheet of fabric, desk lamps

Procedure:

1. "Listen to my piece of music and tell me what kind of action could go along with music?" (If children are ready, teacher can link this to action verbs.)
2. Play track.
3. Discuss answers (traveling).
4. "If this is traveling music, and the character is going somewhere, how does the music tell us that? Listen again and tell me what you think."
5. Play track.
6. Discuss answers (fast, a character who moves to music like this has a very urgent task to carry out).
7. "This piece of music comes from a tiny island in Southeast Asia called Bali. We cannot see it now, but this music goes along with a very special kind of puppet show called shadow puppetry. They make very beautiful puppets that are flat. They put them on sticks and move them around. The puppets are behind a white screen with light shining on them so all you see is their shadow. Did you ever make a shadow shape out on the playground? Check out my video clip to see how these interesting puppets move!"
8. "Let's listen again and you may try to move and dance like the puppets do—pretend your arms and legs move just like the puppets."
9. Play track.
10. Invite children to imagine their own stories and to make a shadow puppet character using the craft supplies listed to tell their stories to the other children using the shadow screen and lights.
11. Extend the activity by creating sonic backdrops for the stories using tone bells or barred Orff percussion instruments.

Music and storytelling go hand in hand—and not just for young children. Program music is a category of musical composition that features some type of extra-musical meaning, portraying an idea, an image, or even a fully developed narrative with music only. No words are involved in telling these stories; the music itself and the listener's imagination combine to create (or re-create) a tale or picture or feeling. Notable works of program music include Ludwig van Beethoven's third symphony in E-flat, the "Eroica" symphony intended to celebrate Napoleon. Hector Berlioz's "Symphonie Fantastique" takes the listener on a wild ride of a journey through the experience of an artist and his obsession with the woman he loves. The impressionistic work of Claude Debussy may be considered programmatic, as well. His piece "Nuage" engages the listener in the swirling sounds of clouds, in perpetual motion, never quite settling, but soft and accessible nonetheless.

Teachers would be correct in their assessment that the scope and content of these aforementioned works are likely to be beyond the grasp of little ones. French composer Camille Saint-Saëns has gifted children and teachers with his programmatic work, "The Carnival of the Animals." The 14 short and accessible movements portray different types of animals or groups of animals, cleverly capturing the spirit of these creatures through orchestration, tempo, and texture. Teachers and children alike will be inspired by the well-crafted and amusing depictions of animals such as a flock of birds in an aviary, jumping kangaroos, fearsome lions, lumbering tortoises, and, of course, an aquarium full of beautiful sea creatures. The "Aquarium" movement is featured here in Episode 6.3, inviting children to engage in storytelling, not simply with words, but with movements.

Episode 6.3: Go Fish! Saint-Saëns's "Aquarium"

(For Integrating)

Specific Use: Ages 4 to 7

Materials:

- "Aquarium," Barry Wordsworth & London Symphony Orchestra, iTunes

Procedure:

1. "Music friends, sometimes music can tell a story without any words at all! Can you think of a way that music could tell you something without any words?"
2. Field answers.
3. "What kind of story could be told with fast, exciting music?"
4. Field answers.
5. "What kind of story could be told with slow, gentle music?"

6. Field answers.
7. "What kind of story could be told with choppy music?"
8. Field answers.
9. "I am going to play a piece of music for you that has a story that goes with it. I will give you a hint: It is about a group of animals, and some of you might even have these as a pet at home. Listen and then tell me which animals you think this could be about."
10. Play track.
11. Field answers.
12. "If you were thinking about fish, then you were correct! This is a piece by a French composer, Camille Saint-Saëns, called 'Aquarium.' What are some things about this music that might make you think of an aquarium full of beautiful fish?"
13. Field answers (slow, quiet, smooth like fish).
14. "Let's help Mr. Saint-Saëns with his storytelling by moving like fish in an aquarium as we listen. Try to tell the story of your fish with your movements only—no talking!"
15. Play track. Invite children to move about the space.

Science

Early childhood science curricula encompass a wide variety of topics and skills. Everything from the basic needs of living organisms to exploration of the five senses can be covered in the early days of viewing the world through a scientific lens. The scientific method might be introduced in a rudimentary way, encouraging children to ask questions and figure out ways to answer them. Children may learn about the environment around them, the ways in which organisms develop and change, the habitats of various wildlife, and the realms of outer space.

Science and music have always gone hand in hand, with the science of sound waves at the root of all our musical perception. Children's natural curiosity about the world serves them well as they investigate the intersection of science and sound. Musical instruments in and of themselves provide meaningful illustrations of the many ways in which the vibrations of sound may be made. Exploring the vibrating air columns of aerophones, the vibrating strings of chordophones, the instrument body vibrations of idiophones, and the vibrating drum heads of membranophones helps children understand the production of sound waves (Figure 6.1). Early childhood learners are capable of grasping the relationship between pitch and size by engaging with a variety of instruments, including the varying sizes of xylophone bars, large and small Boomwhackers, pan pipes, and more, as pictured in Figure 6.4.

An aspect of science that is appealing to just about every child is that of the study of animals. Animals are part of their daily lives as they care for pets, play with stuffed animals, collect animal toys, consume animal-shaped snacks, view animal characters in cartoon programs, and read stories featuring animal protagonists. Many children are very excited to share their knowledge of and preference for animals with others—this topic provides a concrete and child-friendly way to connect various aspects of children's lives. Consider the Learning Pathway piece "Moli Hua," which tells of the jasmine flower and its nocturnal tendencies. Episode 6.4 helps children connect the nocturnal nature of the jasmine with many of their favorite animals.

Episode 6.4: The Gentle Jasmine: A Chinese Melody (Learning Pathway #2)

(For Integrating)

Specific Use: Ages 3 to 6

Materials:

- "Moli Hua," Crystal Children's Choir & Karl Chang, iTunes, photographs and facts about nocturnal animals

Procedure:

1. "Can you remember an interesting fact about the jasmine flower? What time of day might you see one?"
2. Discuss answers (petals unfold at nighttime).
3. "So we know about a plant that we might see at nighttime. Do you know of any animals that you might only see at nighttime?"
4. Discuss answers (raccoon, bat, owl, coyote, firefly, fox, gray wolf, etc.).
5. "These animals are called nocturnal because they like to be awake during the night and asleep during the day."
6. Show photographs and share facts about various nocturnal animals.
7. Extend this activity by inviting children to draw their favorite nocturnal animal as they listen to "Moli Hua."

Aside from the physical aspects of sound, the wonders of science find their way into many types of musical expressions. Many cultures use music and sound to celebrate nature, to give thanks for the fruitful land, or to acknowledge the mysteries of the physical universe. The meteorological phenomenon of rain is common to the artistic lives of cultures all over the globe. Episode 6.5 invites young children to consider the water cycle, using the soulful sounds of Ladysmith Black Mambazo as a backdrop for interpretive movement. Dedicated to the preservation of South African lore and musical traditions, Ladysmith Black Mambazo has captivated the world for over half a century with their ebullient choral tones and harmonies. This piece becomes all the more beautiful when one realizes the scarcity of rain in some regions of South Africa.

Figure 6.1 Exploring pitch and instrument size in hands-on ways

Episode 6.5: Rain, Beautiful Rain: Ladysmith Black Mambazo and the Water Cycle

(For Integrating)

Specific Use: Ages 4 to 6

Materials:

- "Rain, Rain, Beautiful Rain," Ladysmith Black Mambazo, iTunes, visual of the water cycle (SmartBoard, felt board, illustrations, etc.)

Procedure:

1. "Listen to my piece of music and tell me what type of weather you are hearing about."
2. Play track.
3. Discuss answers (rain).
4. "What are some reasons that rain is important?"
5. Discuss answers (gives water to plants and animals, fills up bodies of water, provides drinking water, fun to play in).
6. Introduce children to the water cycle: condensation (water is stored up in clouds), precipitation (water falls to the earth as rain), collection (water is

stored in lakes, rivers, streams, oceans), evaporation (water goes back up into the clouds as a gas).

7. Invite children to come up with a movement for each component of the water cycle that demonstrates its function within the process. For example, precipitation might involve using fingers as rain drops to cascade gently to the ground.
8. Perform movements to "Rain, Rain, Beautiful Rain."

It is not uncommon for young children, at the start of the school day or during a daycare morning circle time gathering, to discuss important data such as day of the week, the month and date, and even the weather outside. Manipulatives help children document and chart their weather assessments, developing awareness of their environments and how the weather may impact day-to-day living in terms of appropriate clothing, travel, or the possibility of outdoor playtime. Children all over the world experience climate and weather in different ways—some may never have seen a single snowflake in person, some may be well acquainted with the possibility and effects of hurricanes, and some may dwell in dry desert air with little interaction with rain. For many children, their home climates might feature weather that changes with the seasons. Perhaps winter brings snow, followed by blossoming warmth in the spring, a hot and sunny summer, and a crisp fall with colorful foliage. Perhaps seasons are less straightforward, with one distinguished from another through increased rainfall. Some may experience winter during different months of the year depending upon their hemisphere of residence. Regardless of the manifestation of seasons and weather, young children begin to develop awareness of their environments in the beginning stages of learning about their world through a scientific lens.

The lesson in Episode 6.6 draws children into the conversation about weather and season with the work of Italian Baroque composer Antonio Vivaldi, composer of the art music staple "The Four Seasons." Each of these four concerti captures the spirit of the season for which it is named: "Spring," "Summer," "Autumn," and "Winter," with programmatic elements that bring each of these to life. Episode 6.6 offers "Winter" as a point of departure, but teachers may wish to include the other concerti as an extension of the lesson or as a follow-up in subsequent lessons. Engaging children with props for movement will help them bring the winter snow to life in this lesson. Teachers may even wish to bring in a snow globe trinket to demonstrate how snowflakes swirl and fall.

Episode 6.6: The Wonder of Winter: Vivaldi's Four Seasons

(For Integrating)

Specific Use: Ages 4 to 6

Materials:

- "Winter, I. Allegro non Molto," Takako Nishizaki, Capella Istropolitana & Stephen Gunzenhauser, iTunes, props for movement such as snowflake cut-outs, white ribbons, or scarves

Procedure:

1. "Raise your hand, music friends, if you would like to tell me what the weather is like outside."
2. Field answers.
3. "Do you see any snow?"
4. Field answers.
5. "You are smart musicians who know that music can sometimes make us think of other things that we experience in our lives. Well, we even have music that sounds like different seasons and weather! We will listen to a piece of music, and afterwards, you can tell me what kind of weather it sounds like to you."
6. Play track.
7. Field answers.
8. "This is part of a piece of music by an Italian composer named Antonio Vivaldi called 'Winter.' Listen again and use your fingers to show the snowflakes swirling around."
9. Play track.
10. "You may use your whole body to show the snowflakes this time!"
11. Distribute movement props.
12. Play track and invite children to dance.

Visual Arts

Many a refrigerator door has been adorned with the artistic endeavors of young children. With paints, crayons, markers, glue, and, to some parents' dismay, glitter that stays for a while and then flakes away and drops to the floor, young children are active in exploring their artistic sides in colorful, visual, and tactile ways. Young children learn early on to employ basic elements of visual arts such as drawing lines and shapes. They are encouraged to use this vehicle as a way to express themselves, to develop their creativity, and to carve out an artistic niche for themselves in the world.

Connecting music and the visual arts follows what is a natural fit for children. Many of the terms used in these art forms are either the same or have analogous partners in the other art form. Both art forms explore texture, form, and color, with melodic contours relating to line, phrasing relating to shape, and the many expressive qualities of music that relate to light and dark. In Episode 6.7, the Learning Pathway selection, "Tera Xylophone," presents a compelling opportunity to investigate the complex rhythmic concept of polyrhythm. Just as sounds are layered upon one another, so can young children manipulate art materials to create a layered work. Teachers should exercise extra patience and caution when using glue with young children!

Episode 6.7: X Marks the Spot: Xylophones of West Africa (Learning Pathway #3)

(For Integrating)

Specific Use: Ages 5 to 7

Materials:

- "Tera Xylophone," Music from the Villages of Northeastern Nigeria, Smithsonian Folkways, paper, pieces of colored tissue paper cut into small squares, glue

Procedure:

1. "We talked about how our xylophone music from West Africa has lots of different layers of sound. We can give that a fancy musical name called 'polyrhythm.' Let's create a piece of art that also has different layers, but instead of layers of sound it will be layers of colors."
2. Demonstrate how to glue pieces of tissue paper to the paper. Layer colors on top of other colors to create new shades and combinations.
3. Distribute paper, tissue paper squares, and glue to children.
4. Supervise and assist as they create their own layered collages.

The ethereal sounds of "Hymn for the Sunrise" draw children into the possibilities of the connection of sound and color. Some individuals experience synesthesia, a condition in which hearing sounds evokes mental images of colors. Finnish composer Jean Sibelius experienced this condition and even had a green-tiled fireplace in his home that he affectionately called the "F Major" fireplace. This artistic glimpse into the music of the Middle East and North Africa is the perfect point of departure for little ones to listen and create. Musical artist and ethnomusicologist Ali Jihad Racy is featured here in Episode 6.8, a master of both wind and stringed instruments of the Middle East. Inspired by the ancient Egyptian Book of the Dead, a guide to navigating the afterlife, Racy's composition uses traditional instruments to bring listeners into the mystical realm depicted by intricate tomb paintings and early writings.

Episode 6.8: Painting the Sunrise: Artistry in the Middle East

(For Integrating)

Specific Use: Ages 4 to 6

Materials:

- "Hymn for the Sunrise," Ali Jihad Racy, iTunes, paper and art supplies such as crayons, markers, colored pencils, pastels, or paints

Procedure:

1. "Listen to my piece of music and tell me what kind of pictures or colors it makes you think of."
2. Play track.
3. Discuss answers (will vary).
4. "This music makes me think of pinks and oranges, and yellows, the colors of the sunrise. Maybe that is why this piece of music is called 'Hymn for the Sunrise.' You might be surprised to know that this piece of music was based on beautiful drawings that ancient people drew on the walls! I bet you are not allowed to draw on the walls at your house!"
5. "Listen to my piece of music again and see if you can tell me where you think it comes from."
6. Play track.
7. Discuss answers (Middle East/North Africa).
8. "Let's use this piece of music as an inspiration for a piece of art. As you create your art, think about what colors the music makes you think of, if you should use gentle or fast strokes to draw/paint, if this is a peaceful or exciting piece of music."
9. Distribute art supplies to children.
10. Play track as children create their art works.

As an aural art form, it is possible that music may sometimes be abstract to young children. They may require visuals or movement to aid in their engagement with music, to help them more fully comprehend the many and varied components of music. Linking music to the visual arts makes good sense in the early childhood years as they begin to express themselves through various artistic media. Many early childhood curricula introduce children to styles of visual art and connect them with the artists of origin. Ancient Greek pottery, Impressionistic paintings, and modern sculpture may all capture the imagination of young children. Consider the visual art connection offered by the set of musical compositions entitled "Pictures at an Exhibition" by Russian composer Modest Moussorgsky. In this suite of pieces originally scored for piano, Moussorgsky has created movements inspired by the visual art of his friend, Viktor Hartmann. Episode 6.9 invites children to work backwards, in a sense, by listening to Moussorgsky's "Ballet of the Unhatched Chicks" and drawing what they might imagine the original work of art looked like. Teachers will want to be prepared to show Hartmann's original sketch featuring people in egg costumes (the planning phases of an Easter parade), as children seem to find it quite amusing. This activity could be a point of departure for interactions with other styles of art from varying time periods or places across the globe.

Episode 6.9: Drawing With Moussorgsky's Music

(For Integrating)

Specific Use: Ages 4 to 6

Materials:

- "Ballet of the Unhatched Chicks," New York Philharmonic & Leonard Bernstein, iTunes, paper and art supplies such as crayons, markers, colored pencils, copy of original Viktor Hartmann egg costume sketch

Procedure:

1. "Music friends, sometimes people who write music are inspired by things they see. They might be inspired by things they see in nature, or in the sky, or even things like pictures and paintings. What are some things that inspire you to make music?"
2. Field answers.
3. "A long time ago a man named Modest Moussorgsky had a very good friend who was an artist. He decided that a nice thing to do for his friend was to write pieces of music that went along with his friend's drawings and paintings. Today, though, you get to be the artist! Let's listen to a piece called 'Ballet of the Unhatched Chicks' and see if you can draw your idea of what the original piece of art looked like!"
4. Distribute art supplies.
5. Play track while drawing.
6. Show drawings and solicit explanations for what the children drew.

Mathematics

Mathematics in the early childhood curriculum addresses many concepts and skills that children must develop in order to be successful not just in higher levels of mathematics, but in life in general. Counting and basic arithmetic are certainly in the mix, but other conceptual aspects of this content area are included as well. For example, young children learn about sequencing and ways to classify and sort objects. They learn about shapes and how to identify and draw them. Patterning is one of the great joys of the early days of math, as young ones delight in both creating patterns and finding them in the various places and spaces of their daily lives. Children learn to compare and contrast and communicate about similarities and differences. These and more lay a solid foundation for future mathematical endeavors.

Mathematics and music are inexorably linked and cannot exist without one another. While music is much more than a method to teach mathematics, young children delight in the connections that can be made. For example, finding a pattern in quarter note and eighth note literacy activities can be a magical discovery. Not only does music invite children to multiply and divide, to count, to create patterns, it invites the consideration of shapes as well and how shapes might translate into ways to notate the things they hear. With roots in European colonialism in America, shape note singing was a method of altering traditional Western music notation in order to make sight singing easier and more accessible (Figure 6.2). Shape note singing is still practiced in contemporary North America, especially in the American south. Episode 6.10 introduces young children to this musical phenomenon.

Episode 6.10: Sharing Shapes: Shape Note Singing in the U.S.

(For Integrating)

Specific Use: Ages 5 to 7

Materials:

- "Singing School," The Social Harp, iTunes, classroom instruments (i.e., rhythm sticks, egg shakers, tambourines, hand drums), sample of shape note notation, whiteboard/marker, crayons, paper

Procedure:

1. "Listen to my piece of music and try to tell me what kind of instruments you hear."
2. Play track.
3. Discuss answers (voices).

4. "Listen again and tell me if you hear all the same kinds of voices or different kinds of voices."
5. Play track.
6. Discuss answers (different kinds of voices, high and low, women and men).
7. "This is a very neat way of singing and writing down music found in the United States called shape note singing. They use different kinds of shapes to show the singers which sound they should make. This way of singing was taught in singing schools which helped beginning singers in the colonial days of America learn how to sing. Let's try singing some of their special patterns. You sing what I sing, please."
8. Sing various tonal patterns using fa, sol, la as per shape note tradition.
9. "What are some of your favorite shapes?"
10. Discuss answers and draw the shapes on the board.
11. "What if we made our own kind of shape notes? Let's use your favorite shapes to decide which kind of instrument sounds can go along with them."
12. Discuss instrument timbres/shapes. For example, square is a rhythm stick, circle is a hand drum, triangle is a tambourine, rectangle is a hand drum.
13. Distribute instruments to children.
14. Play the adapted shape notes.
15. Invite children to create their own compositions. Distribute crayons and paper for students to draw their shapes.
16. Perform student compositions.

Young children delight in learning to count and demonstrating this skill to others. While teachers and caregivers may comprehend the counting that underlies music, such as counting rhythms or counting measure of rest, children can join in on counting beats. The experience in Episode 6.11 brings children into the realm of American mid-twentieth century jazz with the standard favorite by Paul Desmond, "Take Five." The Dave Brubeck Quartet has long been associated with this piece as the ensemble featured on the original recording. Children will not be able to help moving along with the unusual meter, feeling groups of five beats per measure. Many early childhood classrooms feature a number or letter of the week—teachers will be all set for five to have a turn!

Figure 6.2 Traditional shape note notation and modified shape note notation for early childhood

Episode 6.11: Fabulous Five

(For Integrating)

Specific Use: Ages 4 to 5

Materials:

- "Take Five," Dave Brubeck, iTunes

Procedure:

1. "Music friends, show me how you count to five!"
2. Children and teacher count together.
3. "Let's count to five and tap once for each number on our laps."
4. Count and tap.
5. "Let's count to five and tap our heads!"
6. Count and tap.
7. "Where can we tap next?"
8. Field answers. Count and tap.
9. "Let's make our counting a bit more interesting with some music."
10. Play track.
11. Children count and tap five beats in different variations as announced by teacher.
12. For a variation, the children can count in different languages.

Even children at the very youngest of ages benefit from hearing and seeing the basic numerals that they will use throughout their lives. They sing along with number songs and view illustrations of numbers in child-friendly books and on educational television programs. The courageous teacher may wish to engage young children in a bit of counting along with the work of American contemporary minimalist composer Philip Glass. Episode 6.12 draws children into the unique sonic world of the opera "Einstein on the Beach," a contemporary theatrical work that deviates from the typical linear storyline of operas. "Knee Play 1" is an intermezzo found within this opera. Teachers can easily display a visual of numbers 1 through 8 and point along as children chant or sing.

Episode 6.12: Clever Counting

(For Integrating)

Specific Use: Ages 2 to 4

Materials:

- "Knee Play 1," Philip Glass Ensemble, iTunes, visuals of numbers 1 through 8

Procedure:

1. Play track and invite children to join in counting.
2. Point to numbers as they are sung in the piece.
3. Optional extension: Give children their own number visuals to follow along and count.

Health/Physical Education/Dance

Physical Education in early childhood learning settings provides an avenue to developing fine and gross motor skills in order to live a healthy and active lifestyle. In this context, children learn how to care for their bodies and how to move safely for themselves and others. They develop balance and coordination in movement while developing a vocabulary of ways to move their bodies in locomotor and nonlocomotor ways.

Music and movement are fused together in ways that can never be separated. Even the act of playing an instrument or singing requires the physical effort of moving one's hands, feet, lips, tongue, vocal cords, brain, lungs, and diaphragm. On a larger scale, many cultures consider music and movement together as one entity, each inseparable from the other. Young children can easily be classified in this way as well, with their almost continual motion and natural instinct to move with music. Few children engage in these physical activities cognizant of the health benefits or physical coordination required. Rather, they play! Play can be a safe entry point into the musical expressions of indigenous North American groups, ensuring that the selection is not to be used for a sacred ritual or rite. The "Play Song" of the Haida tribe of British Columbia can be an inspiration point for children to connect to others through play and to design their own musical playscapes. This pentatonic tune in Episode 6.13 is also easy for children to sing along to and can even open doors to improvisatory endeavors.

Episode 6.13: We All Play! Music of Indigenous North America

(For Integrating)

Specific Use: Ages 5 to 6

Materials:

- "Play Song," Haida: Indian Music of the Pacific Northwest, Smithsonian Folkways

Procedure:

1. "Music friends, can you tell me what kinds of musical games you know?"
2. Field student answers (will vary, for example, "Ring Around the Rosy," "London Bridge," handclapping games, jump rope songs, etc.).
3. "People all over the world use music to play—even grown-ups! Here is a piece of music for you to listen to. Please listen carefully and tell me what kind of game you might imagine playing to this kind of music."
4. Play track.
5. Field student answers.
6. "Let's create a game that can go along with this piece of music and play it together."
7. Guide children in creating a game. Possibilities include a handclapping game, a counting out game, a duck, duck, goose style game, a chase game, etc.

Teachers and caregivers may find that a great deal of music that is marketed toward children in a commercial sense offers little variety in the way of musical meters. Children may grow up to a duple sonic backdrop, never feeling any other way to organize music and movement. During these formational years, however, young children should most definitely hear and respond to music featuring a multiplicity of ways to feel or divide metrical beats. In order to engage young children successfully in musical movement in non-duple meters, teachers must be sure to choose music that very clearly demonstrates the selected meter. A compelling example of music for movement in triple meter is "Fanny Power," an Irish folk tune composed in the 18th century after a real woman of the same name. This tune featured in Episode 6.14 has been passed down for generations and has been played on many a fiddle and tin whistle. This recording featuring traditional Irish musicians is distributed by Comhaltas, an organization dedicated to preserving and transmitting Irish music and Irish cultural traditions. As the children prepare to move, the teacher may wish to provide a movement prop such as a scarf or ball or bean bag to allow children to differentiate between the strong downbeat of each measure and the lighter beats two and three.

Episode 6.14: Metrical Movement

(For Integrating)

Specific Use: Ages 5 to 7

Materials:

- "Fanny Power," Comhaltas, iTunes, props for movement such as balls, scarves, bean bags, etc.

Procedure:

1. "Music friends, please listen to my piece of Irish music and stay seated while you just move how the music makes you feel like moving."
2. Play track and move along.
3. "Good work. Now let's try moving to the music like this—we will pat our laps once and then do two claps. Let's try: pat clap clap, pat clap clap. Please try this with the music."
4. Play track while performing the pat clap clap pattern.
5. "Good job again! Now you may get up and find your own space in the room to move. As you move, try to remember which parts of the music felt like pats and which felt like claps. Try to move differently for those two parts of the music."
6. Distribute movement props if desired.
7. Play track and move freely.

Young children are constantly on the move! They bop and wiggle and scoot and gallop and run. While they may be quite skilled at vigorous movement, they may need some support when it comes to moving slowly and fluidly. Teachers can encourage this way of moving in Episode 6.15 with the Chinese piece entitled "Chatting With an Old Friend by the Window," a lyrical tune featuring the traditional instruments of the stringed *erhu* and bamboo flute. The traditional sounds are juxtaposed with the more contemporary and global piano, perhaps indicating that musical traditions continue to develop and morph and integrate timbres from other cultures.

Episode 6.15: Chatting With an Old Friend

(For Integrating)

Specific Use: Ages 5 to 7

Materials:

- "Chatting With an Old Friend by the Window," Chinese Bamboo Flute, iTunes, red Stop sign and green Go sign

Procedure:

1. "Music friends, please find your own space in the room. Make sure you are not in anyone's space but your own."
2. Assist children with finding a movement space.

3. "You are all good runners and dancers and jumpers and wigglers! Today, I wonder if you can show me how good you are at moving slowly and gracefully, too. When I show you this red Stop sign, your job is to freeze like a statue. When I show you this green Go sign, your job is to move gently just how the Chinese bamboo flute is playing."
4. Play track.
5. Alternate Stop and Go signs in accordance with the phrasing of the music.

Social Studies

Social Studies in the early childhood setting encourages young children to get to know the world around them, both close to them and far from them. Studying the self, family, community, and world at large helps them develop a sense of where they belong. Content of Social Studies integration lessons may include exploration of community helpers, cultural symbols such as flags, and basic map-reading skills.

Music and Social Studies may combine in interesting ways for the early childhood setting. World Music Pedagogy exists to open the ears of children to the world around them, making music a perfect vehicle for exploration of their local and global surroundings. In order to set the stage for learning about musical cultures of the Andes mountains, a musical story can be employed. Storytelling and books are wonderful ways to encourage childhood literacy and capture and maintain attention, all the while introducing young ones to various musical cultures in a child-friendly way. *Carolina's Gift* is a storybook by Katacha Díaz that tells the tale of a young Andean girl seeking just the perfect birthday gift for her grandmother (*abuelita*). Carolina heads to the village market and is dazzled by the many traditional crafts, spectacular colors, delicious foods, festive music, and interesting animals, but she still did not find something just right for her special grandmother. At last, she finds a carved wooden walking stick that will allow *abuelita* the mobility to accompany Carolina to the market! Children enjoy taking the trip along with Carolina and even enjoy singing the interspersed tune "looking for a gift for *abuelita*" on sol sol mi la sol mi (see Figure 6.3). Discussion with young children following this story can be quite rich and illuminating. Questions and prompts such as, "How does Carolina's home look the same or different as yours?" or "How does the place where Carolina shops for *abuelita* look the same or different as where you shop with your family?" can be quite effective in opening up a dialogue about cultural observations and comparisons.

Featured in Episode 6.16, the Peruvian tune "El Condor Pasa," by Daniel Alomia Robles, is an excellent way to introduce children to the sonic possibilities of Andean music. Combining *Carolina's Gift* with engagement with this well-known song can help teachers and students more effectively establish and understand the context in which real live people make (and make meaning of) music and the instruments they use to do so (Figure 6.4). The study of this region of the world may be extended in Episode 6.17 through the traditional song and folk dance "Viva Jujuy" (pictured in Figure 6.5). This tune is essentially a love song for one's homeland and presents opportunities for young children to both glimpse the values of traditional Andean peoples while reflecting upon the things they love about their own homes. "Kon Kon" in Episode 6.18 provides an aural glimpse into the musical celebrations of indigenous Andeans featuring the traditional drum, *caja*, and the traditional flute, *rayán*. Teachers may wish to combine the following three episodes in order provide young children with a multimodal Andean encounter.

Episode 6.16: El Condor Pasa: Peruvian Possibilities

(For Integrating)

Specific Use: Ages 5 to 6

Materials:

- "El Condor Pasa," Flute Music of the Andes, iTunes, map of South America, *Carolina's Gift* storybook, panflute (real instrument or photograph), charango (real instrument or photograph)

Procedure:

1. "Listen to my piece of music and see if you can guess the type of instrument you hear."
2. Play track.
3. Discuss answers (a type of flute).
4. "There are different types of flutes all over the world. This flute is called a *siku* and comes from South America." Show instrument.
5. Point to South America on the map. Point to where the children are from and compare the distance. How could you get there? By car, boat, airplane, or on foot?
6. "Listen again and see if you hear another instrument."
7. Play track.
8. Discuss answers (charango, a stringed instrument). Show instrument.
9. "This is a very important piece of music from the country of Peru, and it is called 'El Condor Pasa.' This means the condor (a kind of bird) passes by. This is a very special song to the people of Peru. What are some songs that are important to people where you are from?
10. Discuss answers.
11. Extend by reading *Carolina's Gift* and discuss life in a traditional Andean village, such as family celebrations, home life, and shopping in a traditional market place.

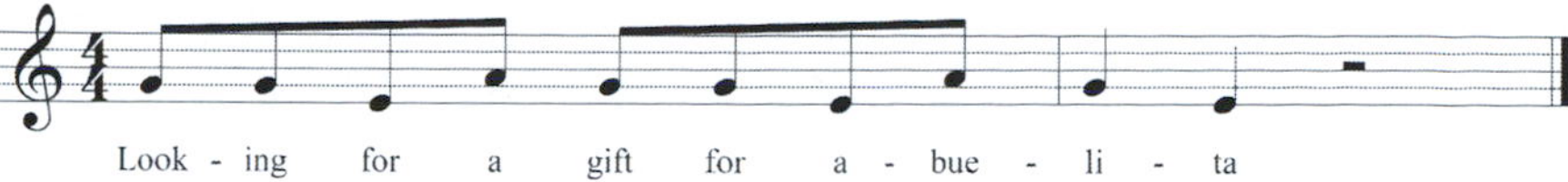
Look - ing for a gift for a - bue - li - ta

Figure 6.3 Recurring tune for *Carolina's Gift*

Episode 6.17: Proud of My Home! Andean Pride Through Music and Dance

(For Integrating)

Specific Use: Ages 5 to 6

Materials:

- "Viva Jujuy," Guarani Songs and Dances, iTunes

Procedure:

1. "Listen to my piece of music and tell me if you think a really fast exciting dance would work best with this music, or maybe a more gentle dance."
2. Play track.
3. Discuss answers (gentle dance).
4. "Stand up in your spot and put the beat of the song in your feet. Show me gentle feet, close to the floor."
5. Play track.
6. "This piece of music is a traditional song from the Andes mountains in South America. People in the Andes region may dance in circle shapes. They may even wear special woven clothing with patterns and colors that show other people what area they are from. Let's try the traditional dance that goes with this piece of music."
7. Form a standing circle, holding hands.
8. Dance maneuvers:
   a. Step into the circle for four beats.
   b. Step back out for four beats.
   c. Rotate circle counterclockwise for four beats.
   d. Let go of hands and do one spin gently in place.
9. "This song is all about being proud of the place you come from, which is something that people in the Andes region have in common with people in other places in the world. What are some things that make you proud of the place you live?"
10. Discuss answers.

Episode 6.18: Festive Flutes and Dramatic Drums

(For Integrating)

Specific Use: Ages 5 to 6

Materials:

- "Kon Kon," Tomás Roque Mendoza, Smithsonian Folkways

Procedure:

1. "Music friends, when you have a celebration in your family or with your school, what kinds of music to you hear there?"
2. Field answers.
3. "People in the Andes mountains have a lot of different celebrations just like you do, and they love to use music to celebrate and dance. Listen to my piece of music and tell me what kind of celebration would use this music."
4. Play track.
5. Field answers.
6. "This music comes from a dance that celebrates good spirits. You probably heard two very special instruments, a drum called a *caja* and a flute called a *rayán*. Let's listen again and try to pat the drum beats on your lap or on the floor."
7. Play track.

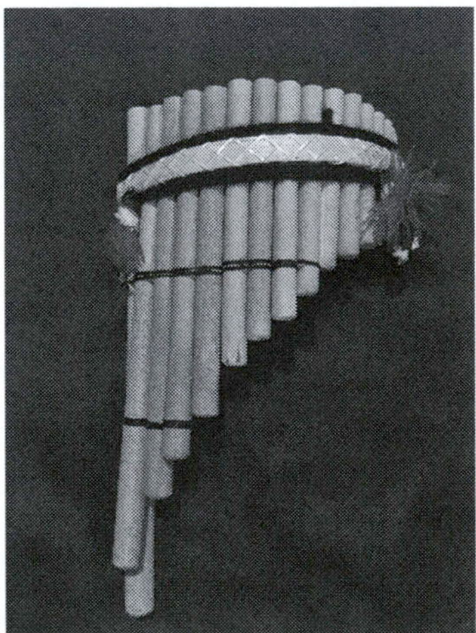

Figure 6.4 Andean panflute

Figure 6.5 Children and their teacher dancing "Viva Jujuy"

Holidays and Celebrations

There is always something to celebrate with young children! From the everyday celebrations of birthdays, lost teeth, and academic achievements to the large-scale cultural celebrations that unite communities, children are ready to soak up the rituals and commemorations of their local and global surroundings. Young children are primed for religious and secular holidays and traditions, ready to enjoy the music, food, decorations, customs, and interactions that come with these cultural celebrations.

With many people across the globe ascribing to Judeo-Christian religious affiliations, the holiday of Christmas is one celebrated the world over, with many and varied manifestations of holiday traditions and rituals. Of Mexican origin, Las Posadas is a Christmas tradition that features the retelling of the Nativity story, of Mary and Joseph traveling to Bethlehem and giving birth to Jesus in a stable. The singing, prayers, and storytelling of Las Posadas take place over the course of the nine nights prior to the Christmas Eve celebration on December 24. Costumed groups sing and process among local homes and are "refused" lodging as were Mary and Joseph during the time of the census in Bethlehem. Finally, the faithful arrive at the designated home and are permitted entry, and food is shared. It is not always easy to explain cultural traditions to young children. However, the children's book, *Uno, Dos, Tres, Posadas!* by Virginia Kroll is a kid-friendly way to introduce little ones to the various components of this tradition, including the preparation of food and flowers, singing, and striking the star-shaped piñata. Episode 6.19 asks children to consider the myriad ways Christmas traditions are celebrated.

Episode 6.19: Las Posadas

(For Integrating)

Specific Use: Ages 4 to 7

Materials:

- "Las Posadas," Music of New Mexico: Hispanic Traditions, Smithsonian Folkways

Procedure:

1. "Music friends, we can learn a lot about people all over the world by exploring their holiday traditions. If you feel comfortable, you may raise your hand and tell us a holiday you celebrate with your family."
2. Field answers.
3. "I am going to play a piece of music for you, and I would like you to listen carefully and tell me which holiday could be celebrated with this music."
4. Play track.
5. Field answers.
6. "If you were thinking Christmas, you were right! A lot of people celebrate Christmas in lots of different ways. Listen again and tell me the kinds of musical instruments you hear that are part of this Christmas celebration."
7. Play track.
8. Field answers.
9. "This music comes from a very special way to celebrate Christmas called Las Posadas. Do you know which language Las Posadas comes from?"
10. Field answers (Spanish).
11. "Many people in Spanish-speaking parts of the world prepare for Christmas by celebrating Las Posadas. Let's find out more about this tradition with this storybook called *Uno, Dos, Tres, Posadas!* Maybe there are some things in this book that you do with your families, too!"
12. Read story.

For many in the world, the winter months usher in the celebration of Chanukah, a Jewish festival commemorating the people of Israel and their defeat of the large invading Greek army. Following the defeat of the Greek army, the people of Israel sought to light the menorah in the Holy Temple. Although there was only enough oil to light the candles for one day, a miracle occurred in which this oil lasted for eight days. Thus, the eight nights of Chanukah commemorate this miracle with a nightly lighting of the menorah, songs and prayers, and special foods. S'vivon is a

Hebrew song frequently sung by children telling of the wonders of Chanukah. Translations vary, but several include mention of the spinning dreidel and the miraculous nature of the origin of the celebration. Young children should be able to join in singing this tune in Episode 6.20 with no problem.

Episode 6.20: Singing S'vivon: Celebrating Chanukah Through Song

(For Integrating)

Specific Use: Ages 4 to 7

Materials:

- "S'vivon," Shiron L'Yeladim: Jewish Songs for Children Ages 6–9, iTunes

Procedure:

1. "Please listen to my song and tell me which holiday celebration might use this piece of music."
2. Play track.
3. Field answers.
4. "This piece of music is called S'vivon, and many children like you sing it during the celebration of Chanukah. During Chanukah, families light candles on a candle holder called a menorah. They do this for eight nights in a row, and they have special songs, prayers, and foods that go along with the celebration. The words of S'vivon are about playing a game with a little spinning top called a dreidel and the miracles that happened a long time ago when the people of Israel needed help keeping their candles lit. Listen to S'vivon again and join in singing when you are ready. The first part of the song is in the Hebrew language, and the second part of the song is in English."
5. Play track. Sing along. Repeat as necessary.

S'vivon Lyrics

S'vivon sov sov sov
Chanukah hu chag tov
Chanukah hu chag tov
S'vivon, sov sov sov

Chag simcha hu la-am
Nes gadol haya sham
Nes gadol haya sham
Chag simcha hu la-am

S'vivon turn turn turn
While the lovely candles burn
What a great holiday
Watch us sing and watch us play

Tell the story everywhere
A great miracle happened there
It's a festival of lights
For eight days and for eight nights

Some people may offer shouts of "Happy New Year!" at midnight on January 1. However, not everyone celebrates the new year in the same way or at the same time. Chinese New Year aligns with the appearance of the new moon between January and February. It is a celebration steeped in traditions such as the cleaning of the home to welcome good luck, family reunions, exchange of red envelopes of money, elaborate dragon dances, consumption of delicious dumplings, exciting fireworks, and, of course, music. The song "Gong Xi Fa Cai" is among the most popular heard during this festive time of year. The translation, "May you be happy and prosperous," speaks to the root of this annual celebration. Young children are sure to be enthralled with the upbeat, contemporary version of this song found in Episode 6.21. Teachers might be interested in the children's storybook *A New Year's Reunion*, by Yu Li-Quiong and Zhu Cheng-Lang, as an extension for this lesson.

Episode 6.21: Gong Xi Fa Cai

(For Integrating)

Specific Use: Ages 4 to 7

Materials:

- "Gong Xi Fa Cai," Tommy Wong, iTunes, lengths of red flowing fabric for movement

Procedure:

1. "Music friends, listen to my piece of music and tell me if this matches with an exciting, happy holiday or a holiday where we should be very quiet and reflect."
2. Play track.
3. Field answers.

4. "It sounds pretty happy to me, too! You might recognize this song, 'Gong Xi Fa Cai,' as part of the Chinese New Year celebrations. What are some ways you celebrate Chinese New Year?"
5. Field answers.
6. "Does anyone know the special color that we see a lot during Chinese New Year?"
7. Field answers (red).
8. "Let's dance with our red fabric to celebrate Chinese New Year! Many dances use fancy dragon or lion props. Can you dance like a dragon or a lion?"
9. Distribute fabric.
10. Play track and dance.

Teacher Feature: Ms. Le Zhang

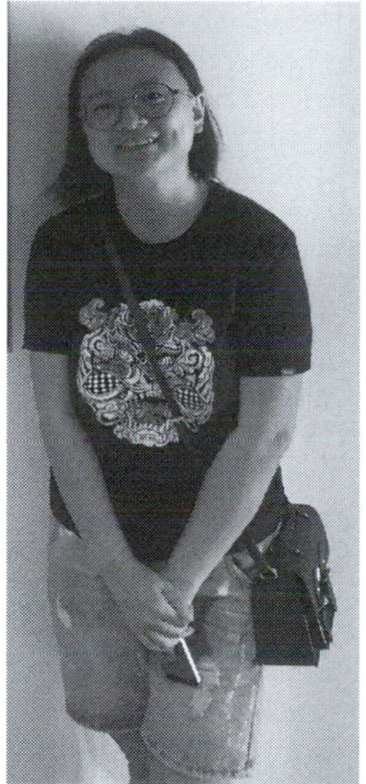

Ms. Le Zhang

Prior to her move to the U.S. to pursue further music studies, teacher and researcher Ms. Le Zhang lived and worked in Beijing, China. She attended a conservatory in the western part of China and majored in voice. Following her studies, she found herself teaching 3- to 6-year-old children in various musical capacities. She laughed that "they express their feelings very directly" and that "they are cute and I enjoy the procedure of teaching them." Ms. Zhang's early childhood music classes can be characterized by variety in listening encounters as well as interpretive movement, singing, playing instruments, and storytelling. She employs techniques of Orff, Kodály, and Dalcroze into her lessons and even explored the possibilities of giving children the opportunity to make some choices in their musicking—a revolutionary choice given the emphasis on teacher-directed instruction and discipline in her school setting in China, but one that has been well-received in her teaching in the U.S. Her story is truly one of the spirit of integration as she has skillfully woven together Chinese and Western music for young children across the globe. To see her in action with Chinese and American students in the classroom is to see this approach unfold with great success—it is clear that her name, "Le," means "happy," for all her students are a reflection of the joy she finds in making music with little ones.

Q: Your teaching seems to be characterized by an interesting integration of Chinese and Western music. You had mentioned that you are using some Chinese folk songs with your children in an American preschool class. Can you tell me about that?
A: Yes, one has same tune as "Are You Sleeping?" but it has Chinese words about two tigers. One has no eyes and the other has no tail. It's weird! I have an English translation, but when I sing to the kids I use the Chinese version. One child in the class that learned this song never talked. He had only been in America for a few months. He had big problems with language. The teacher was very worried about him because he never talked or communicated with anyone. Only nodding or gestures. Very, very quiet. The first time I entered this class, the teacher communicated his language struggles to me. I remember thinking maybe he can't find a friend, so I taught them all greeting words. That day we sang the two tiger song. This child was very excited and tried to join in. The teachers cried after class! That was the first time in a whole month this child talked. Sometimes the teacher needs to do something to make the kids feel safe and special in a new culture. That's why I decided to volunteer to work with them. Every Friday I have lunch with [the Chinese speaking children]. I ask them about their week and if they missed me. Do you think I'm a beauty? Yes, I'm beautiful, I know. They are very excited, "A big friend comes just for me!"

Q: It's great that you are using songs and language to connect with children both of Chinese and Western cultures. Children who have moved to the United States from China may be in a strange place, but they get a taste of home through your music. What about the children who are not Chinese speaking? How do they respond to your Chinese folk songs?
A: They think my songs are very interesting. Sometimes they say "what!?" just like that. They are trying to sing with me, I can tell. I predicted that when I would sing a Chinese song the American kids would be angry or would laugh at me, but it totally shocked me that they liked it. I think for the kids everything is the same! I can do whatever, English, Spanish, French, and they will like to sing the song. I think this is different from Chinese kids. I had a Chinese child in class who didn't know English, and when he heard a song in English he got angry. "I don't want to join this! I want to go home!" I found a lot of details that are different about American kids.

Q: In what other ways to engage young children in music, integrating areas of interest to little ones?

A: Every class we will have a topic. For example, the topic of "cats." It will have some relevant songs, games, music, activities about cats and mice, movement and dance. Another class might be about bears, in the mountains, different kinds of bears, grandma bear, grandpa bear, and different instruments to represent them. We use the xylophone to imitate the stomping of the bears. In each class we have a hello part and a goodbye part and a core part that contains the activities and games related to the topic.

Q: How are young children listening to music in your classes?
A: We have some different levels of listening. The first level might be listening to the teacher's singing. If we want to show the kids [a concept], the teacher will sing for them. Then we invite the kids to follow, just like in the hello song or goodbye song or some new songs we want kids to learn with us. The other level is training their voice. In this stage, we invite the kids to do what we do, just like a normal [rote procedure] exercise. We use the kazoo to invite the kids to imitate the teacher. The other level is we invite the kids to do some movement after they've heard the music. For example, if a class topic is the wind, we don't tell the kids, "This music is about the wind." We show them first and let them guess. We provide them with scarves, plastic bags, or paper [for movement props]. After this they have the flexibility to choose instruments they like to match the music they heard. In this procedure, the students can follow the music, choose the instruments they like, and play as a group and with the teacher. I remember one of the pieces of music was called "Bear Family." In this music we had different kinds of bears. We tell the kids first, "This is about a special animal and you can guess what it is!" Some kids will guess, "This sounds like a huge animal!" And we'll say, "Wow! That's right! A huge dog or giant or elephant?" They can do specific movements to match the baby or mom or grandpa bear. They adjust movements to pitch and tempo of the different bear family members.

Q: You have taught music to young children in China and in the U.S. Can you speak to how those experiences have been different? Or have they?
A: Yes. I think they are quite different! I sometimes wonder why they are so different, but then I think of the backgrounds of the teachers. In China, the maximum degree for Kindergarten teachers is the bachelor's degree. The majority of them do not have that. Because of this, the Chinese teacher will implement traditional teaching methods. The Chinese teacher would like all the children to keep quiet and listen to the teacher. We even use movement and gestures to control the behaviors. A very noisy and crowded classroom can be quiet in just a few seconds. In American classrooms, the teachers do not want to control the children's actions through discipline. They will have a lot of flexibility to express and to ask questions and to make their own choices. In China, the majority of things are decided by the teacher.

Q: You've been working with American children in a music setting since you moved here. What has that been like as a Chinese teacher, working with children who might be accustomed to having a bit more choice and autonomy?
A: Before I taught these children I was nervous because of the language. I think the children's language is totally different from my professors and classmates. They can't speak very clearly. Sometimes the words sound like completely different vocabulary than what I have heard! There is a lead teacher in the preschool class I teach. She stays there to help me. The kids are very interested in Chinese things. One third of them can

speak Chinese. I think in my teaching, I start from teaching in half Chinese and half English. I try to teach them some Chinese vocabulary like fruit or animals. I volunteered in this class before so the kids know me. I think this helped me to know them. They like having me as their music teacher. I can totally ignore the discipline thing [because the lead teacher is there]!

Q: What would you recommend to non-Chinese teachers who would want to use some traditional Chinese music in their teaching?
A: I think you can choose familiar tunes as a starting point, like "Twinkle, Twinkle" or "Are You Sleeping?" These songs are familiar to both Chinese and American children. Just change the words.

Q: If I wanted to teach a Chinese song or listen to Chinese music that did not have a common tune, where could I start?
A: The first thing is to get familiar with this song, to find some video of this music to study. Find songs with activities or games that go with them—this is a familiar thing to do with music. Some songs they can be encouraged to sing, not everyone will be able to do this 100%, but the ones who are familiar can be leaders. Add games and activities to songs as children get to know them.

Q: What about using Chinese traditional music for listening activities?
A: Chinese traditional instrumental music is very special and beautiful. You can choose some pictures of traditional instruments to show to them and let them imagine how they sound. Then you can play the music for them and let them guess which instrument made that music. They can even imitate the instruments with their voices. The first step is to play games with the music. I always play games with them and use the music as the background and then teach them about the melody, then the rhythm, then let them analyze the content. The final aim is to learn to sing the song!

Bringing It All Together

Young children have a unique way of making all aspects of their lives musical—at work and at play, their rhythmicking, singing, humming, dancing, and wiggling pervade their daily activities. They are natural integrators, bringing music into their surroundings completely on their own. Teachers can take this instinct even further by connecting music with the other content areas children are exploring in their schooling and home lives. Rooted in the listening experiences of the World Music Pedagogy process, integrating takes children to the next level, encouraging to embrace the music of others as their own.

References

Brown, M. W. (2012). *Around the world we go!* Bath, UK: Parragon.

Carolan, T. (2008). *Old Makana had a taro farm*. Kauai, HI: Banana Patch Press.

Diaz, K. (2002). *Carolina's gift: A story of Peru*. Norwalk, CT: Soundprints.

Kroll, V. & Lopez, L. (2006). *Uno, dos, tres, Posadas!* New York, NY: Puffin Books.

Li-Qiong, Y. & Cheng-Lang, Z. (2007). *A New Year's reunion*. Somerville, MA: Candlewick Press.

Listening Episodes—Learning Pathways

"Anoai," Jacob Feuerring with Tom Hiona, Smithsonian Folkways, *hula kahiko* featuring *'uli 'uli* gourd rattles www.folkways.si.edu/hawaiian-dancers-male-singer/anoai-hula-uliuli/hawaii/music/track/smithsonian

"Moli Hua," Crystal Children's Choir & Karl Chang, iTunes, choral arrangement of traditional Chinese melody https://itunes.apple.com/WebObjects/MZStore.woa/wa/viewCollaboration?cc=us&ids=431607970-431607973

"Tera Xylophone," Music from the Villages of Northeastern Nigeria, Smithsonian Folkways, traditional xylophones of West Africa www.folkways.si.edu/music-of-the-tera-people-tera-xylophone-music/world/music/track/smithsonian

Listening Episodes

"Wayang Sasak: Rangsang," Sekaha Sekar Karya, Smithsonian Folkways, Balinese gamelan music accompanying shadow puppetry www.folkways.si.edu/sekaha-sekar-karya/wayang-sasak-rangsang/islamica-world/music/track/smithsonian (www.radioaustralia.net.au/international/2014-03-18/introducing-indonesian-culture-through-shadow-puppets/1281172)

"Aquarium," Barry Wordsworth & London Symphony Orchestra, iTunes, excerpt of "Carnival of the Animals" https://itunes.apple.com/us/album/carnival-of-the-animals-vii-aquarium/50864568?i=50864092

"Rain, Rain Beautiful Rain," Ladysmith Black Mambazo, iTunes, South African vocal ensemble https://itunes.apple.com/us/album/shaka-zulu/id302138028

"Winter, I. Allegro non Molto," Takako Nishizaki, Capella Istropolitana & Stephen Gunzenhauser, iTunes, Vivaldi's "Winter, Movement I," from the "Four Seasons" https://itunes.apple.com/us/album/the-4-seasons-winter-i-allegro-non-molto/394109385?i=394109441

"Hymn for the Sunrise," Ali Jihad Racy, iTunes, Middle Eastern classical music https://itunes.apple.com/us/album/hymn-for-the-sunrise/id49312343?i=49312257

"Ballet of the Unhatched Chicks," New York Philharmonic & Leonard Bernstein, iTunes, movement of Moussorgsky's programmatic work, "Pictures at an Exhibition" https://itunes.apple.com/us/album/pictures-at-an-exhibition-v-ballet-of-the-unhatched-chicks/908799588?i=908799670

"Singing School," The Social Harp, iTunes, traditional American shape note singing https://itunes.apple.com/us/album/singing-school/id2459157?i=2459105

"Take Five," Dave Brubeck, iTunes, jazz standard in unusual meter https://itunes.apple.com/us/artist/dave-brubeck/545242

"Knee Play 1," Philip Glass Ensemble, iTunes, contemporary theatrical composition https://itunes.apple.com/us/composer/id98277385

"Play Song," Haida: Indian Music of the Pacific Northwest, Smithsonian Folkways, social music for play www.folkways.si.edu/mungo-martin/mm-44-play-song/american-indian/music/track/smithsonian

"Fanny Power," Comhaltas, iTunes, traditional Irish tune in triple meter https://itunes.apple.com/us/artist/comhaltas/289200123

"Chatting With an Old Friend by the Window," Chinese Bamboo Flute, iTunes, piece featuring Chinese bamboo flute and *erhu* https://itunes.apple.com/us/artist/chinese-bamboo-flute/146646660

"El Condor Pasa," Flute Music of the Andes, iTunes, famous Andean piece for traditional flutes and voice https://itunes.apple.com/us/album/el-condor-pasa/id844787705?i=844787782

"Viva Jujuy," Guarani Songs and Dances, iTunes, traditional Andean song and folk dance https://itunes.apple.com/us/album/v%C3%ADva-jujuy/id128056814?i=128055974

"Kon Kon," Tomás Roque Mendoza, Smithsonian Folkways, traditional Andean dance featuring flutes and drums https://folkways.si.edu/tomas-roque-mendoza/kon-kon/latin-sacred-world/music/track/smithsonian

"Las Posadas," Music of New Mexico: Hispanic Traditions, Smithsonian Folkways, musical celebration of the Christian Nativity https://folkways.si.edu/coro-de-san-jose/las-posadas/american-folk-gospel-latin/music/track/smithsonian

"S'vivon," Shiron L'Yeladim: Jewish Songs for Children Ages 6–9, iTunes, children's song for Chanukah https://itunes.apple.com/us/album/svivon/310988941?i=310989000

Gong Xi Fa Cai," Tommy Wong, "iTunes, popular Chinese New Year song https://itunes.apple.com/us/album/gong-xi-fa-cai/1321830775?i=1321831181

7

Surmountable Challenges and Worthy Outcomes

The world is shrinking every day—through technology, travel, access, and innovative ways to connect, citizens of the world are closer in touch than ever. While music may be practiced, enjoyed, or perceived in different ways, music as an aural art form remains a thread that unites all people. As such, music is a compelling point of entry for young children to learn about themselves and others, the cultures, peoples, lifeways, traditions, sounds, and sights that link humanity. World Music Pedagogy offers an accessible path for teachers of children from birth on to the beginnings of formal schooling to bring the sounds of the world's musical cultures into the places and spaces where young children can begin to appreciate and understand themselves, their relationship with others in the world, and, of course, the musical expressions that are so rich and varied. Using this systematic method, teachers can proceed with confidence and enthusiasm, knowing they are working to enhance young children's awareness of culture in and through music.

Benefits of World Music Pedagogy in Early Childhood

Social and Cultural Benefits

The benefits of World Music Pedagogy in the early childhood setting are many and varied and are congruent with skills, content, and dispositions already found in many early childhood curricular programs. For example, social and emotional intelligence are frequently and intentionally developed both in the home and in early childhood learning and care centers. Early childhood curricula may focus on building empathy from an early age, being able to envision the lives and experiences of others. World Music Pedagogy supports this goal through exposure to many different sounds and contexts accompanied by careful questioning to help little ones put themselves into the "shoes" of others, understanding lifeways, values, traditions, and customs of others across the globe, leading to the development of dispositions of acceptance, tolerance, respect, friendship, and love. Appropriate communication is also emphasized in early childhood curricula, with teachers encouraging children to draw upon their own vocabularies to tell others how they feel or what they are thinking.

Activities and encounters from the preceding chapters point to the cultivation of social and emotional intelligences. "E Komo Mai," in Chapter 2, invites children to explore different facial expressions, determine the relevant emotion, and make a connection to the music they hear. Even if they do not all match the music with the same emotion, they are still tackling the process of thinking about their own feelings in response to music and interpreting the feelings of others. Emotional intelligence is developed through exercises such as these where children are given tools and techniques to express themselves.

Key aspects of social learning in the early childhood years include learning self-regulation and sharing. The music teaching and learning process is ripe with opportunities to apply these very important social skills. For example, the "Tutuki" episode, in Chapter 5, invites children to improvise on a xylophone. It could very well occur that the number of available xylophones is fewer than the number of children in the lesson group—in this case, little ones get a first-hand taste of the sharing and community spirit required to make music. Sharing and self-regulation are vital to the creation of music. In the early childhood years, this may mean the sharing of instruments as previously mentioned or simply accepting, without complaint, a certain color of scarf or ribbon even if it is not their preference.

Imaginary play is an important part of the early childhood years and can most certainly be developed through World Music Pedagogy. For example, the tune "Con Voi" from Vietnam featured in Chapter 2 might inspire children to move about the room like elephants—animal imitation is a favorite activity among small children. The Learning Pathway piece featured throughout the volume, "Moli Hua," invites children to use scarves to represent the jasmine blossom unfurling and recoiling, engaging the kinesthetic imagination in a playful way. Add into the mix the exploration of the cultural contexts of these pieces, and children's imaginations are fully engaged with the wonder of different people and places and sounds.

Musical Benefits

The musical benefits of World Music Pedagogy are innumerable, as children learn new musical vocabularies through experiences in listening to, participating in, performing, and creating music of the world's cultures. These encounters with new and different sounds enable young children to build an aural memory bank, making connections to their own diverse repertoires as they learn and hear new things. In this way, music is most certainly a vehicle for expanding little ones' thinking and perceptions of the manifestations of diversity through music and cultural understanding.

Children in the early years of life are musical sponges, soaking up sounds and creating a multitude of their own. World Music Pedagogy offers an interesting way to cultivate the musical skills and knowledge that young children are already exploring. Healthy and appropriate use of the singing voice is an emergent skill throughout the early years of life, and World Music Pedagogy provides infinite ways to develop this skill. In Chapter 3 of this volume, the Anglo-American children's song by Pete Seeger, "Bought Me a Cat," invites children to both sing along and explore the capabilities of their voices through animal sound exploration. They engage their personal instrument, experiencing the lightness of the head voice and the heaviness of the chest voice—and the joy in using the voice just for fun! As a Learning Pathway selection across the dimensions of World Music Pedagogy, "Moli Hua" presents children with an opportunity to sing this Chinese melody in the native language or simply on a neutral syllable as a way to enjoy singing a beautiful tune unfettered by unfamiliar pronunciations. The voice is an easy avenue to instant musical participation and involvement with myriad ways to put it to use.

Musical movement is crucial for early childhood music learners, and the world's musical cultures are full of opportunities to get up and put those motor skills to work! Many of the world's cultures fuse music and movement into a single entity, with the two always existing in an interconnected way. Young children are developing in terms of fine and gross motor skills but should still be given the opportunity to try out new approaches to engage their bodies in musical ways, even if the result is not perfectly timed or executed. This volume provides starting points for teachers and caregivers to facilitate movement in many ways, some as simple as using body percussion to feel a beat or tap a rhythm pattern. The Learning Pathway selection "Anoai" invites children to use body percussion to perform the simple *'uli 'uli* pattern before transferring to an instrument. The Hawaiian tune "E Pele Pele Pele" (Chapter 3) and Latin jazz selection "Oye Como Va" provide children with kinesthetic opportunities that merge with the exploration of iconic notation (Chapter 5) by tapping their fingers on various shapes and patterns that assist them in fine motor musicking. The folk dances and passing games within this volume present more challenging movement opportunities for children who are ready (and teachers who are courageous). Young children are always on the move, exploring their space and pushing the limits of their bodies—World Music Pedagogy capitalizes on this desire to move while making the world a bit smaller at the same time. Movement is not simply just a tool, however. Movement in the musical realms of many cultures is fully integrated into the musical act. To move is to do the music wholeheartedly.

Many of the activities featured in this volume involve young children in the exploration of musical instruments. Not only are they listening and developing sensitivities to instrumental timbres from the world's musical cultures, they are also getting their hands on some real instruments. Playing and improvising on child-friendly instruments such as Orff xylophones, rhythm sticks, hand drums, and tone bells sets children up for engaging fully in a musical sense, but also to realize the rules of instrument technique and care. Passing and trying authentic examples of musical instruments from around the world proves to be particularly fascinating for young children as these encounters bring real-life artifacts of musical cultures right into the presence of little ones.

World Music Pedagogy is rooted in listening, but most certainly extends into the realm of creativity. A musical benefit of this process is the opportunity to bring children into the space of musical creativity, improvising with voices and instruments within appropriate contexts and even finding ways to compose their own sounds and movements. Many young children may not have models of musically creative people in their lives—World Music Pedagogy cultivates a creative spark from early on, instilling young children with the notion that music is something they actively do.

Children come into the world prepared to learn, to make sense of the demands of early life in ways that are meaningful to them. They learn about themselves, about their families, their friends and neighbors, and the wider world beyond, layer by layer and experience by experience, from close to far. They become comfortable with their own identity and grow in curiosity about the ways of others. They observe, watch, listen, and sense from their environments and caregivers how to employ language, how to interact with others, how to behave, and the values of those in their social circles. They are immersed in their multi-sensory worlds and are primed to engage in the process of learning about the world's musical cultures simply because of how they already interact with the world. The immersive experience of a young child, his oral and aural observation of the world, is similar in many facets to the ways in which the world's musical cultures teach and learn music.

Worthwhile Challenges

Teacher (Self) Education

Engaging young children in the World Music Pedagogy process is truly a worthwhile endeavor, but not one without challenges. First and foremost a teacher may face challenges within herself, before even stepping in front of children. It can be daunting to launch one's self into the study of the music of another culture, to overcome fears, anxieties, biases, and judgments to become immersed in the unfamiliar. The level of study required to represent even one musical culture appropriately is not insignificant—this takes a commitment of time and energy on behalf of the teacher. Consultation of resources recommended within the episodes makes a great start into World Music Pedagogy and ways of opening young children to the musical riches of the world. The teacher owes this potential discomfort and growth to herself and to her students—getting outside of one's comfort zone and pushing one's self musically in many directions results in a bank of teaching repertoire and strategies that are far more inclusive, global, and meaningful.

For the hesitant teacher, it might be most useful to start with herself, taking some time to reflect upon her own culture and branching out from these questions: What types of music have served important roles? How does music connect to the teacher's family heritage? How is music integrated into holidays and celebrations? What can be comfortably shared with children and connected with stories, artifacts, and accessible music? Can the teacher demonstrate an instrument or a dance or a song in the native language of her culture of origin? Does the teacher have any friends or family members who might demonstrate musicking of their heritage as culture-bearers? It is important for the teacher to recall that she is connected to culture herself, which might present a doorway into empathetically exploring and teaching the cultures of others. Her own journey may serve as a model to little ones that learning about the wide diversity of people in the world is truly a lifelong endeavor.

Teachers may wrestle with issues such as authenticity and representation and may question the validity of bringing the world's musical cultures into their teaching. Some may be tempted to forego this process altogether for fear of being disrespectful of a culture or misappropriating a musical selection. The informed teacher embraces the challenge, however, with sensitivity and intelligence. It is unlikely that a teacher would be able to load all of her children onto a plane to fly to South America and witness first-hand the musicking of a feast day in Cusco, Peru. The teacher must commit to doing the research and developing the resources that will bring that feast day or other cultural entity to life for the children in her classroom as closely as possible. The children are better off learning through a carefully crafted lesson than never hearing of the myriad ways people make music worldwide. All involved benefit from this endeavor—the children develop a sense of interconnectedness through music while the teacher continues to develop herself as a musician and educational professional.

Little Kids Are Little!

Once the teacher is appropriately prepared and ready to incorporate World Music Pedagogy into the various manifestations of early childhood music education, she must consider the variability of early childhood music learners themselves. The adept teacher of this age group knows to expect the unexpected and to be flexible and present, in the moment. A difficult transition from the classroom, a sudden and necessary diaper change, or a poor night's sleep can all easily impact a young child's engagement and disposition. Even if a world music encounter might not be executed perfectly, it is often the imperfections that make working with young children so compelling.

The World Music Pedagogy process involves the oral tradition, in which listening to music is a cornerstone of knowing the aural soundscapes across the globe. World Music Pedagogy makes use of many iterations of short listening segments—perfect for the developmental attributes of young children. As in many of the episodes from this volume, only short examples are presented to the children; they will likely be bursting to share their thoughts after only a few moments, anyway!

Although not essential to the World Music Pedagogy framework, young children may be able to listen for longer periods of time if the teacher implements a visual or focus object of some type. Focus objects for listening might include listening maps, photographs, charts, graphs, puppets, instruments, or anything that captures the imagination of the teacher and the children. As she progresses through the World Music Pedagogy process with young children, the skilled teacher will balance and blend listening with playing and participation so as to keep young children engaged while setting the stage for more sophisticated musical listening in the future.

Planning Encounters in World Music Cultures for Young Children

World Music Pedagogy is intended as a framework for opening the ears, eyes, and minds of learners in music and through music to the brilliance of human diversity and to the ways in which people across the planet express their cultural identity. It is a road map with specific suggestions for ways to unite the very best insights from ethnomusicology, music education, multicultural education, and early childhood studies, and it is a means for offering young children opportunities to experience equity in knowing many musical cultures through means that fit their learning capacities from infancy, through toddlerhood, the preschool years, and Kindergarten. The chapters are full of strategies for bringing the musical world close to young children so that they may develop sensitivity, skills, and understandings in music and in the human relationships they can have from an early age onward.

Each music teacher will have his or her own preferences as to how to build these World Music Pedagogy experiences into music classes or lessons for young children. The following segments provide some points of departure for piecing together musically and culturally compelling lessons for the delight of little ones. Early childhood teachers and caregivers can shape these suggestions into daily circle times and classroom routines and transitions, as well as in full-fledged lessons.

The Components of a Typical Session

Chapter 3 posited various suggestions for musicking effectively and successfully with little ones, suggestions that teachers will want to bring into their careful planning of World Music Pedagogy encounters. For example, young children thrive on routine, which smart teachers can capitalize upon in their music instruction. This is not to say that each and every class session is structured in exactly the same way, but consistency in the types of musical engagement offered to children builds rapport, trust, and comfort with full participation. Many early childhood music classes begin with some type of welcome or greeting song intended to signal to the children that music time is officially beginning. This song of welcome may include instruments or movement or incorporate student contributions and suggestions—the possibilities are both fun and endless. For example, in a greeting song that involved playing egg shakers in different kinds of ways, a group of Kindergarteners suggested saying hello in the various languages spoken by members of the class.

Following a hello song might be some type of warm-up activity, just a short song or game that invites children to-move a bit. “Simama Kaa” makes a wonderful warm-up as it is a simple tune with easy-to-learn Swahili lyrics along with ups, downs, and jumps. Children love to play this game at various tempi (especially fast!) and love to connect with other children in the world who also enjoy playing lively games. Other warm-ups might include a collection of culture-specific rhymes, chants, fingerplays, or vocal explorations, drawing upon the potentials of East Asia, West Africa, South America, Northern Europe, Island cultures of the Caribbean and Pacific, and beyond.

In order to reflect the importance of storytelling in the world’s cultures, teachers can include stories told in musical ways. Many works of children’s literature are structured in rhyming phrases, perfect for chanting rhythmically and patting a steady beat. Other stories might have repeating words and phrases that lend themselves to singing on a simple melodic figure or adding elements of vocal exploration. Stories might be told with actual storybooks, felt board manipulatives, interactive whiteboard manipulatives, puppets, dolls, movements, and more. The incorporation of musical storytelling into early childhood music lessons is beneficial for children and teachers for many reasons, not the least of which are supporting early childhood literacy goals, providing a point of focus for children who need it, and, simply put, the fun of children’s literature! Additionally, bringing musical stories into young children’s musical encounters is a masterful way to further develop children’s cultural knowledge and awareness of the contexts from which their world music lessons are derived. Many are the times a child has latched on to a favorite story, begging before bedtime, “Read it again!” It seems, then, that the use of musical stories to illuminate the world’s musical cultures is a natural fit.

Further lesson components might include sequences with manipulatives such as child-sized instruments or class sets of finger puppets. Placing a musical instrument or puppet friend into the hands of a child can be vital to unlocking their confidence and willingness to fully engage in music instruction. Combine these with listening and movement and magic will unfold! When a teacher does not have enough instruments to go around, she might implement a "focus instrument" session, in which the children take turns experimenting with a special instrument. The Learning Pathway selection "Anoai" would lend itself well to such a session; all children could be participating, playing the *'uli 'uli* pattern on kid-friendly egg shakers while they take turns playing the real *'uli 'uli*.

Closing an early childhood music class signals to the children that music time is ending and that a transition is impending. Again, this issue of routine, bookending the lesson with hello and goodbye songs, invites children into a musical space in a friendly way and finally indicates that it is time to move on to other activities. This can certainly happen in a multicultural way—the early childhood favorite of "See Ya Later Alligator" features many different ways to say goodbye through various slang sayings and other languages. While this might not be considered a substantive aspect of the World Music Pedagogy repertoire, it can be a fun connection point for children to learn bits of the languages of the cultures they are exploring

Tools for Planning and Preparation

Teachers of young children may find the following organizational tool featured in Table 7.1 useful in their preparations for implementing music lessons for this age group. This grid is set up for once-per-week class meetings with children, but of course it can be adapted to the needs of practicing teachers who may choose to feature music sessions daily, or three times weekly, or as appropriate for their settings. While this planning grid order does not, of course, need to be strictly adhered to in every lesson, it does give the teacher a point of departure for ensuring that different

Table 7.1 Planning grid for early childhood music lesson units

	Session 1	*Session 2*	*Session 3*	*Session 4*	*Session 5*	*Session 6*
Hello song						
Warm-up						
Finger puppet sequence						
Listening						
Movement						
Musical story						
Musical instrument						
Goodbye song						

modes of music learning and the various stages of the World Music Pedagogy process are being facilitated both within single lessons and across time. Using the aforementioned lesson segments, this planning grid might take some of the guesswork out of crafting engaging lessons for early childhood. Teachers can customize within this structure, ensuring that they are weaving Attentive Listening, Engaged Listening, Enactive Listening, and experiences in Creating World Music and Integrating World Music into these sessions. Perhaps each session includes one component of the World Music Pedagogy framework, building towards a performance at the culmination of the unit. Teachers may also elect to combine multiple phases into each session, carefully scaffolding young children's exposure in ways that best suit their needs and abilities.

Each and every one of these lesson components presents an occasion to incorporate an aspect of World Music Pedagogy. A hello song or warm-up might include a greeting song with movement from Ghana. A finger puppet sequence might feature an animal indigenous to a particular region of the world along with songs and games from the accompanying culture. Listening, movement, and storytelling are all ripe with possibilities for featuring music of the world's cultures as demonstrated throughout this volume. Engaging with instruments, whether of the classroom or culturally authentic variety, draws children into the kinesthetic realities of how many types of music are made. Songs of farewell are found throughout the world, and teachers can customize their goodbyes to any particular musical culture under study.

Short-Term and Long-Term Encounters With World Music Pedagogy

Using the planning grid presented prior, the following are examples of what both short-term and long-term applications of this sequence might look like when World Music Pedagogy enters the picture. Short-term encounters can be implemented as standalone, single sessions and feature the musical cultures of the Andes mountains, the American phenomenon of shape note singing, or Caribbean steelpan. The long-term

Table 7.2 A single session plan for music of the Andes region

Hello song	"Hello, How Are You?" (Figure 7.1)
Warm-up	"Juego Chirimbolo," South American singing game (Figure 7.2)
Listening (attentive)	Flute music of the Andes, "El Condor Pasa," iTunes, famous Andean piece for traditional flutes and voice (Chapter 6), https://itunes.apple.com/us/album/el-condor-pasa/id844787705?i=844787782
Musical story	*Carolina's Gift* by Katacha Diaz with sung refrain (Chapter 6)
Movement (engaged-enactive)	Guarani songs and dances, "Viva Jujuy," iTunes, traditional Andean song and folk dance (Chapter 6), https://itunes.apple.com/us/album/v%C3%ADva-jujuy/id128056814?i=128055974
Musical instrument	Andean siku (panpipe) (for passing and examination only)
Goodbye song	"See Ya Later Alligator" (Figure 7.3)

encounters, featuring the Learning Pathway selections, present teachers with points of departure to expand the first session into deeper explorations.

SHORT-TERM ENCOUNTER: MUSIC OF THE ANDES REGION

Figure 7.1 Hello song

Figure 7.2 "Juego Chirimbolo"

Figure 7.3 Goodbye song

SHORT-TERM ENCOUNTER: THE SOCIAL HARP AND AMERICAN SHAPE NOTE SINGING

Table 7.3 Single session plan for American shape note singing

Hello song	"Hello, How Are You?"
Warm-up	"Open Shut Them"—American singing game with motions (Figure 7.4)
Listening (attentive)	The Social Harp,"Singing School," iTunes, traditional American shape note singing (Chapter 6), https://itunes.apple.com/us/album/singing-school/id2459157?i=2459105
Musical instrument (creating)	Distribute rhythm sticks, tambourines, and hand drums. Craft felt shapes to display on the felt board to correspond with the following sounds: Rhythm Sticks Tambourines Hand Drums Place shapes in groups of four or eight on the felt board and invite students to perform their instruments at the appropriate times.
Movement (engaged)	"I'm Going Home," free movement with scarves or ribbons, https://itunes.apple.com/us/album/original-sacred-harp/id257160491
Musical story	*So-me Goes Missing* by Stuart Manins (This story connects the solfege heard in the shape note tradition to a loveable character named So-me. Children can sing along with the sol-mi interval when this character's name appears in the story.)
Goodbye song	"See Ya Later Alligator"

Figure 7.4 "Open Shut Them"

SHORT-TERM ENCOUNTER: STEELPAN MUSIC AND FROGS OF THE CARIBBEAN

Table 7.4 Single session plan for frogs of the Caribbean

Hello song	"Hello, How Are You?"
Warm-up	"Simama Kaa"
Finger puppet sequence	Frogs: Vocal exploration with Frogs
Listening	The Invaders, "Coqui," Smithsonian Folkways programmatic steelpan piece about a frog (Chapter 5), www.folkways.si.edu/the-invaders/coqui/caribbean-world/music/track/smithsonian
Movement	"Coqui," free movement with scarves
Musical story	*Freddie the Frog and the Thump in the Night* by Sharon Burch
Goodbye song	"See Ya Later Alligator"

LONG-TERM ENCOUNTERS: HAWAI'I

Teachers of early childhood music may be presented with the opportunity (and luxury) to be able to engage young children in a more long-term exploration of one of the world's musical cultures. Consider the following session that brings children into the musical world of Hawai'i and the subsequent ideas for expanding this encounter into a more long-term endeavor.

The first lesson in this sequence brings children into the sound world of the Hawaiian Islands by encouraging them to listen to the storytelling and chanting of

Table 7.5 Point of departure plan for long-term encounters with Hawaiian music

Hello song	"Hello, How Are You?" (Insert "Aloha, pehea 'oe?" to sing these words in the Hawaiian language)
Warm-up	"Open Shut Them"—singing game
Listening (attentive)	Jacob Feuerring with Tom Hiona, "Anoai," Smithsonian Folkways, *hula kahiko* featuring *'uli 'uli* gourd rattles (Chapter 2)
Movement (engaged-enactive)	The Barefoot Natives, "E Komo Mai," iTunes, contemporary Hawaiian recording group (Chapter 2), activity followed by free movement with scarves, https://itunes.apple.com/us/album/e-komo-mai/id649285502?i=649285804
Musical story	*Old Makana Had a Taro Farm* by T. Carolan
Musical instrument	*'uli 'uli* (one set to pass, play, and share)
Goodbye song	"See Ya Later Alligator"

the Learning Pathway selection "Anoai," as well as the contemporary Hawaiian artists The Barefoot Natives, who perform the listening and movement selection, "E Komo Mai," and provide the accompanying musical track to the story, *Old Makana Had a Taro Farm*. As noted in the grid, the children's encounter with Hawai'i includes singing, Attentive Listening, and Engaged Listening, as well as opportunities to explore storytelling and fundamental aspects of traditional Hawaiian culture.

Teachers can expand this first encounter by, very simply, progressing through the Learning Pathway episodes linked to the hula mele "Anoai." Young children will find themselves along a path of linking rhythmic patterns to body percussion and instrument play in Engaged Listening and Enactive Listening, composing rain-like soundscapes in Creating-Improvising, and using the mele as a point of departure for their own storytelling in Integrating World Music. Teachers can also include the hula mele "E Pele Pele Pele" from Chapter 3 for an additional Engaged Listening experience.

LONG-TERM ENCOUNTERS: CHINA

The following lesson grid presents teachers with a launch pad for bringing a taste of traditional Chinese culture into their early childhood practice. The Learning Pathway selection "Moli Hua" serves as a point of departure for attuning young children's ears to the sounds of China.

The first taste of the long-term encounter brings young children into the sonic world of China, with many possibilities for singing, moving, and playing. A hello song launches the session and is followed by a warm-up activity that assesses children's pitch-matching abilities. The Koo Koo Bird is a new friend that eats beautiful singing voices! Crafted from a cup, children may feed Koo Koo by singing "koo koo" on the sol-mi interval. Children may alert the teacher that they would like to feed Koo Koo by extending their arm to look like a tree branch. When Koo Koo

Table 7.6 Point of departure plan for long-term encounters with Chinese music

Hello song	"Hello, How Are You?"
Warm-up	Koo Koo Bird (Provide a cup with a beak and eyes. Koo Koo Bird eats beautiful singing voices. Children feed him by singing "koo koo" on sol-mi to the bird. When he eats voices, he grows feathers for the next class.)
Listening	Crystal Children's Choir & Karl Chang,"Moli Hua," iTunes, choral arrangement of traditional Chinese melody (Chapter 2), https://itunes.apple.com/WebObjects/MZStore.woa/wa/viewCollaboration?cc=us&ids=431607970-431607973
Movement	The Handkerchief Game from the song collection *Roots and Branches*
Musical story	*The Pet Dragon* by C. Niemann
Musical instrument	Rhythm sticks
Goodbye song	"See Ya Later Alligator"

spots a safe landing space, he descends and is "fed" by the child. Koo Koo is a very motivating presence as he grows new feathers each week, the result of the delicious singing voices he consumed. The Koo Koo Bird sets children up to access the light, lilting head voice register they will need to successfully sing along with "Moli Hua" in future encounters. Attentive Listening with "Moli Hua" invites children to listen and determine what this gentle tune may be about. The Handkerchief Game from the song collection *Roots and Branches* is a "duck, duck, goose" style game in which children can try to tag their friends, to the sonic backdrop of a culturally authentic song game. Teachers and children alike will enjoy the possibilities found within *The Pet Dragon*, a lovely story that weaves characters from the Chinese language into the tale. Following up with some child-sized instrument activities rounds out the lesson—rhythm sticks are suggested here, but any appropriate instrument can substitute. Teachers can play patterns for children to copy or allow children to improvise with their instruments.

Spinning this sequence into future encounters that are more long-term in nature can be quite accessible by following the World Music Pedagogy process through the Learning Pathways. This first session introduces "Moli Hua" through Attentive Listening but can proceed along the continuum as Engaged Listening has them moving in the way of the jasmine flower petals and Enactive Listening invites their singing into the mix (Figure 7.5). Creating and Improvising is on the horizon, as well, with

Figure 7.5 Moving freely with a scarf

the opportunity to compose a nighttime soundscape reflective of the jasmine's nocturnal unfurling. Integrating World Music gives children a scientific view of the piece as they consider other creatures that inhabit the nighttime along with the jasmine flower.

LONG-TERM ENCOUNTERS: AFRICA—EAST AND WEST

It is unfortunate that African cultures are frequently lumped together into one continental mega-culture, without the benefit of immersion into the many and varied places and spaces that make up this continent. The following session provides a starting point for teachers to open up children's ears to the many sounds of the Eastern and Western parts of Africa. The skillful teacher will engage students in brief notes about where in Africa each of the selections comes from, noting that this large continent features many kinds of people and many kinds of music.

Following a song of greeting, children jump right into East Africa with the singing game "Simama Kaa," a meaningful way to relate to the kinds of joyful jumping games children play across the globe. Young children are keenly curious about animals and love to play with individual lion finger puppets. Teachers can utilize these lion friends for vocal exploration purposes or to engage young children in listening games in which they must discern loud music from soft (either performed live by the teacher or recorded), linking the lions to the various forms of wildlife found across the continent of Africa as well as the featured musical story, "The Lion on the Path." Attentive Listening to the "Tera Xylophone" of Nigeria sets children on their journey of developing a concept of the sounds of West Africa. Next, they can further explore West Africa through the Ghanaian song game "Si Si Si," where creativity and instruments combine to allow children some autonomy in their play.

Teachers of young children have many choices for extending these initial encounters into the long-term. The Learning Pathway piece "Tera Xylophone" takes children

Table 7.7 Point of departure plan for encounters with East and West African music

Hello song	"Hello, How Are You?"
Warm-up	"Simama Kaa"—singing game
Finger puppet sequence	Lions —Vocal exploration with lions —Lions dance to loud music, rest for soft music
Listening (attentive)	Music from the Villages of Northeastern Nigeria,"Tera Xylophone," Smithsonian Folkways, traditional xylophones of West Africa (Chapter 2)
Movement (creating)	Kojo Fosu & Edwina Hunter, "Si Si Si," Smithsonian Folkways, African children's counting out game (Chapter 5), www.folkways.si.edu/kojo-fosu-and-edwina-hunter/si-si-si/childrens/music/track/smithsonian
Musical story	"The Lion on the Path" from *The Singing Sack* by H. East
Goodbye song	"See Ya Later Alligator"

through the Engaged Listening encounter of applying body percussion to the various rhythms of the piece, while Enactive Listening invites them to play these patterns on Boomwhackers and tone bells. Improvisation enters the scene as young children use their Boomwhackers and tone bells to create their own accompaniments to the original xylophone piece. Children will delight in combining music and visual art in the Integration phase, crafting a layered collage to reflect the many layers of sound in West African music. Teachers can draw the children south, as they explore the South African song "Rain, Rain, Beautiful Rain," discussing the importance of precipitation in caring for the land.

Exploring diasporic elements of music of the African continent may also be of interest to teachers. The Attentive Listening of "Walk Together Children" in Chapter 2 brings young children into the world of the African American spiritual, an opportunity to connect the vocal sounds with those heard in their previous listening experiences. Further, teachers can connect the Caribbean steelpan tune "Coqui" and the Puerto Rican/American tune of "Oye Como Va" to the various musical elements and instruments that have origins in the continent of Africa (Figure 7.6).

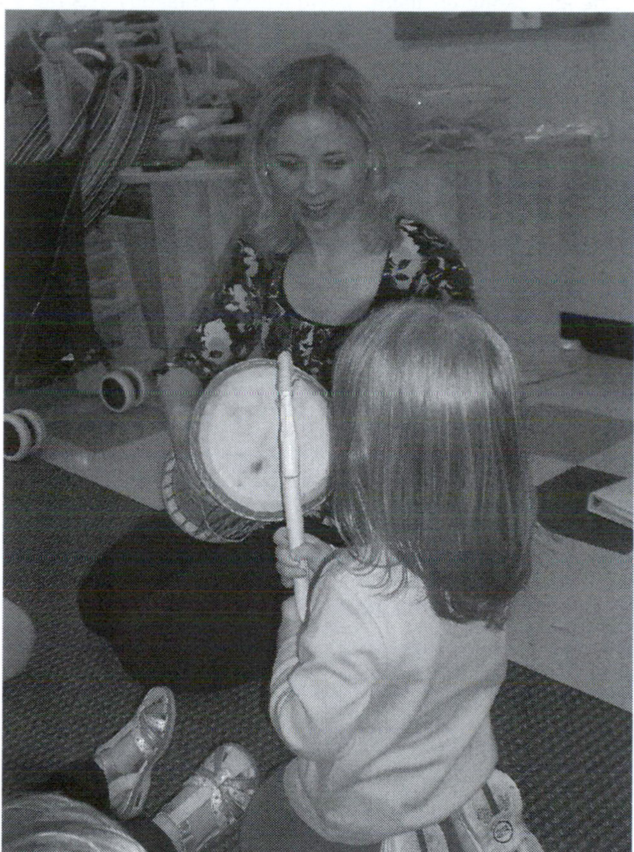

Figure 7.6 Experimenting with a talking drum

The World Awaits!

While there are many challenges in preparing to effectively facilitate encounters for young children in the world's musical cultures, the benefits are truly outstanding. Coming from a place of knowing the developmental characteristics of young children, teachers can build truly impactful learning encounters that open doorways to global understanding and musical appreciation. The World Music Pedagogy process through Attentive Listening, Engaged Listening, Enactive Listening, and experiences in Creating World Music and Integrating World Music provides a foundational way for teachers to effectively plan and implement these encounters with the world's musical cultures for young children.

Music permeates the many and varied threads of human life, a state of affairs that is no different for young children. The early childhood years are a time of rapid and remarkable growth in terms of cognition, language, motor skills, social skills, identity development, and musicianship. This formative period is an ideal time frame for developing not only the aforementioned entities in and through music, but developing a sense of global others, of diversity, inclusion, connecting to others, and actively knowing and caring for them. World Music Pedagogy sets the stage for this worldly consciousness, inviting young children into the musical and cultural tapestry of human interconnectedness and artistic expression.

Reference

Campbell, P. S., McCullouth-Brabson, E., & Tucker, J. C. (1994). *Roots and branches: A legacy of multicultural music for children.* Danbury, CT: World Music Press.

Listening Episodes—Learning Pathways

"Anoai," Jacob Feuerring with Tom Hiona, Smithsonian Folkways, *hula kahiko* featuring *'uli 'uli* gourd rattles www.folkways.si.edu/hawaiian-dancers-male-singer/anoai-hula-uliuli/hawaii/music/track/smithsonian

"Moli Hua," Crystal Children's Choir & Karl Chang, iTunes, choral arrangement of traditional Chinese melody https://itunes.apple.com/WebObjects/MZStore.woa/wa/viewCollaboration?cc=us&ids=431607970-431607973

"Tera Xylophone," Music from the Villages of Northeastern Nigeria, Smithsonian Folkways, traditional xylophones of West Africa www.folkways.si.edu/music-of-the-tera-people-tera-xylophone-music/world/music/track/smithsonian

Appendix 1

Learning Pathways

Learning Pathway #1

Lehua Blossoms in the Rain

Lehua Blossoms in the Rain: Hawaiian Musical Storytelling

(For Attentive Listening)

Specific Use: Ages 3 to 6

Materials:

- "Anoai," Jacob Feuerring with Tom Hiona, Smithsonian Folkways, photograph of lehua blossom, set of *'uli 'uli* or photograph, egg shakers

Procedure:

1. "This piece of music is about something that happens with the weather. Listen and try to figure out what type of weather this might be about."
2. Play track.
3. Discuss answers (rain).
4. "You heard an instrument called the *'uli 'uli*. It is a type of shaker made from a gourd and has different colors of feathers on the top. The sound of the *'uli 'uli* might make us think of little rain drops falling down."
5. Show photographs of *'uli 'uli* or the real instruments.
6. "Listen again and tell me if you hear another kind of instrument."
7. Play track.
8. Discuss answers (voice).
9. "Yes! Your voice is a kind of musical instrument that is inside your own body. You might be surprised to know that in Hawai'i they say this voice is a 'chanting' voice instead of a 'singing' voice. Can you listen again to this chanting voice and see what else you can tell me about the person?"
10. Play track.
11. Discuss answers (chanter has a man's voice, is a grown-up, answers will vary).
12. "Listen one last time and use your fingertips to show the sounds of the rain."
13. Play track.

Lehua Blossoms in the Rain: Hawaiian Musical Storytelling

(For Engaged Listening)

Specific Use: Ages 3 to 6

Materials:

- "Anoai," Jacob Feuerring with Tom Hiona, Smithsonian Folkways, photograph of lehua blossom, set of *'uli 'uli* or photograph, egg shakers

Procedure:

1. "Listen and try to show the rhythm of the *'uli 'uli* somewhere in your body, like your hands, feet, or shoulders."
2. Play track.
3. "This is a very special kind of music called a hula mele. It is a kind of music that tells a story. The story in this piece is about the rain drops gently falling on a lehua flower."
4. Show photograph of lehua blossom.
5. "Let's try to listen again to the rhythm of the *'uli 'uli* and put that rhythm into body percussion like this: pat pat pat pat-pat."

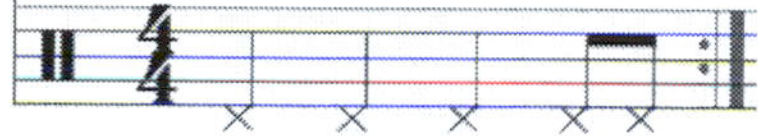

6. Play track.
7. Perform body percussion movements along with track.
8. "Let's listen and put the *'uli 'uli* rhythm in our hands like this: clap clap clap clap-clap."
9. Play track.
10. Perform body percussion movements along with track.
11. "Let's try putting the *'uli 'uli* pattern in our feet like this: stomp stomp stomp stomp-stomp."
12. Play track.
13. Perform body percussion movements along with track.
14. "This time you may put the *'uli 'uli* pattern wherever you like! Maybe you will tap your head or snap your fingers or rub your tummy! You get to choose!"
15. Play track.
16. Perform body percussion movements along with track.

Lehua Blossoms in the Rain: Hawaiian Musical Storytelling

(For Enactive Listening)

Specific Use: Ages 3 to 6

Materials:

- "Anoai," Jacob Feuerring with Tom Hiona, Smithsonian Folkways, photograph of lehua blossom, set of *'uli 'uli* or photograph, egg shakers

Procedure:

1. "Try to remember our song about the rain gently falling on the lehua blossoms. We learned about the *'uli 'uli* that makes the sound of the rain. Listen and do your body percussion movements to the *'uli 'uli* part."
2. Play track.
3. Perform pat pat pat clap-clap body percussion movements.
4. 
5. "Does the *'uli 'uli* remind you of any other instrument you have played before?"
6. Discuss answers (shakers, maracas, etc.)
7. "Let's play our body percussion part on egg shakers so we can sound just like the *'uli 'uli.*"
8. Distribute egg shakers to children.
9. Play track.
10. Play the ta ta ta ti-ti pattern on egg shakers.
11. Extend this activity by inviting children to try the basic hula vamp step of kaholo.

    Step right—touch-step right-touch
    Step left—touch-step left-touch
    Repeat

Lehua Blossoms in the Rain: Hawaiian Musical Storytelling

(For Improvisation)

Specific Use: Ages 3 to 6

Materials:

- "Anoai," Jacob Feuerring with Tom Hiona, Smithsonian Folkways, classroom instruments as available (suggested: rain stick, shekere, glockenspiel, hand drums with small round plastic beads inside for making swirling sounds, cabasa, thunder tube)

Procedure:

1. "Music friends, you may remember our piece of music from Hawai'i that was about the rain and how it fell gently onto the lehua blossom petals. What did you hear that helped you think about rain?"
2. Field student answers (the sounds of the shakers, *'uli 'uli*).
3. "Let's try some different ways to make rain sounds to accompany 'Anoai.' You can make some rain sounds using body percussion! (Snap fingers gently, rub palms together, pat legs quickly, stomp feet for heavy rain.)
4. Play track and improvise body percussion rain sounds.
5. "We can also use some instruments to help us improvise the sounds we hear when it rains."
6. Model and distribute instruments, which might include rain sticks, shakers of various sizes and shapes, ocean drums or hand drums flipped over with small beads to roll around inside, or thunder tubes.
7. Play track and allow children to improvise with their instruments.

Lehua Blossoms in the Rain: Hawaiian Musical Storytelling

(For Integrating)

Specific Use: Ages 3 to 6

Materials:

- "Anoai," Jacob Feuerring with Tom Hiona, Smithsonian Folkways, art supplies such as crayons, markers, paints, etc.

Procedure:

1. "One of the very special things about Hawaiian hula meles is that they are ways to tell stories using words, instruments, and dance. What are some other ways to tell stories?"
2. Discuss answers (movies, books, comic strips, etc.).
3. "Let's use our Hawaiian piece as a story starter. 'The rain fell onto the lehua blossoms and then . . .'"
4. Children complete the story prompt with their own ideas. While the possibilities are endless, children may also be prompted to work within some of the cultural matters of Hawaiian sensibility, such as reverence of the land or loyalty to family.
5. Invite children to illustrate their stories and use their artwork as a scaffold in retelling their stories.

Learning Pathway #2

The Gentle Jasmine

The Gentle Jasmine: A Chinese Melody

(For Attentive Listening)

Specific Use: Ages 3 to 6

Materials:

- "Moli Hua," Crystal Children's Choir & Karl Chang, iTunes, photograph of jasmine flower/vine, sun and moon visuals, scarves/ribbons for dancing

Procedure:

1. "Listen to my piece of music and tell me if this is a very gentle piece of music or a very fast, exciting piece."
2. Play track.
3. Discuss answers (gentle).
4. Listen again and see what you can tell me about this music that sounds gentle to you."
5. Discuss answers (tempo, timbre, dynamic level).
6. "This is a Chinese song about a flower called a jasmine blossom. Flowers are fragile, so it makes sense that this is a gentle piece of music."
7. "Listen again and try to do a two-finger tap to the sounds of the singers' voices."
8. Play track.
9. Observe/assess tapping to melodic contour.

The Gentle Jasmine: A Chinese Melody

(For Engaged Listening)

Specific Use: Ages 3 to 6

Materials:

- "Moli Hua," Crystal Children's Choir & Karl Chang, iTunes, photograph of jasmine flower/vine, sun and moon visuals, scarves/ribbons for dancing

Procedure:

1. "We listened to a piece of music from China about a special thing we would see in nature. Can you remember what it is?"
2. Discuss answers (flower).
3. "This piece is about a very special kind of flower called a jasmine. It does something very interesting. The petals of the flower open at nighttime and close up in the daytime. Let's listen to the voices and the *erhu* try to move like the jasmine flower does."
4. Help children find their own standing spaces in the room. Invite them to move how they think a blooming flower would look at night. Invited them to move how the petals would close during the day.
5. "Let's try your jasmine flower motions with the music. When you see me hold up the sun that means it is daytime and your petals will close up. When you see me hold up the moon that means it is nighttime and your petals will open up."
6. Play track. Display sun and moon, children move accordingly.

The Gentle Jasmine: A Chinese Melody

(For Enactive Listening)

Specific Use: Ages 3 to 6

Materials:

- "Moli Hua," Crystal Children's Choir & Karl Chang, iTunes, photograph of jasmine flower/vine, sun and moon visuals, scarves/ribbons for dancing

Procedure:

1. Play track. Display sun and moon visuals to prompt children's movement.
2. "You have all done such a good job moving like the jasmine flower does during different times of day. Here is what this song means in English."

3. Read translation.
4. "You have heard this song enough times to try to sing along! If you have trouble saying the Chinese words, you may sing on the word 'loo' until you get them."
5. Play track. Sing along.
6. Help children find their own space in the room.
7. Distribute scarves or ribbons for movement.
8. Children may sing along to the melody and then move freely during the interludes.

English Translation

What a beautiful jasmine,
What a beautiful jasmine,
Fragrance and beauty fill every branch.
Fragrant and white, everyone praises it.
Let me pluck for you.
To give to others.
Jasmine, Jasmine.

The Gentle Jasmine: A Chinese Melody

(For Creating)

Specific Use: Ages 3 to 6

Materials:

- "Moli Hua," Crystal Children's Choir & Karl Chang, iTunes, classroom instruments (child-selected), paper or whiteboard for documenting "notation" of soundscape

Procedure:

1. "Music friends, you have done a great job learning about the Chinese song 'Moli Hua' in lots of different kinds of ways. You remember that the jasmine only blooms at which time?"
2. Field student answers (nighttime).
3. "What are some other sounds you hear at nighttime?'
4. Field student answers (will vary—may include insects, wind, rain, traffic, or even imagined sounds). Make a list on the board.

5. "Let's decide what kind of instrument sounds or voice sounds or body percussion sounds could match these ideas. Let's also decide on a way we can show that sound with a picture."
6. Discuss.
7. "Let's decide which one of these should go first, second, and so on."
8. Determine an order.
9. "All right, music friends! We are ready to play our nighttime composition along with our piece, 'Moli Hua.'"
10. Play track. Play notated soundscape. Repeat/adjust as desired.

The Gentle Jasmine: A Chinese Melody

(For Integrating)

Specific Use: Preschool through Kindergarten

Materials:

- "Moli Hua," Crystal Children's Choir & Karl Chang, iTunes, photographs and facts about nocturnal animals

Procedure:

1. "Can you remember an interesting fact about the jasmine flower? What time of day might you see one?"
2. Discuss answers (petals unfold at nighttime).
3. "So we know about a plant that we might see at nighttime. Do you know of any animals that you might only see at nighttime?"
4. Discuss answers (raccoon, bat, owl, coyote, firefly, fox, gray wolf, etc.).
5. "These animals are called nocturnal because they like to be awake during the night and asleep during the day."
6. Show photographs and share facts about various nocturnal animals.
7. Extend this activity by inviting children to draw their favorite nocturnal animal as they listen to "Moli Hua."

Learning Pathway #3

X Marks the Spot

X Marks the Spot: Xylophones of West Africa

(For Attentive Listening)

Specific Use: Ages 5 to 7

Materials:

- "Tera Xylophone," Music from the Villages of Northeastern Nigeria, Smithsonian Folkways, photograph of West African xylophone

Procedure:

1. "Listen to my piece of music and try to figure out what kind of instrument you are hearing."
2. Play track.
3. Discuss answers (xylophone).
4. "Listen again and see if you can tell me how many people are playing together."
5. Play track.
6. Discuss answers (one, although it might sound like more!).
7. "Where in the world do you think this xylophone comes from? Listen and try to figure it out!"
8. Discuss answers (West Africa, Nigeria).
9. "Listen one last time and try to pat a steady beat to the music."
10. Play track.
11. Observe/assess beat keeping.

X Marks the Spot: Xylophones of West Africa

(For Engaged Listening)

Specific Use: Ages 5 to 7

Materials:

- "Tera Xylophone," Music from the Villages of Northeastern Nigeria, Smithsonian Folkways, Boomwhackers (Ab, Db, Eb), tone bells (Db, Eb, F, Ab, Bb), photograph of West African xylophone

Procedure:

1. "Listen to my xylophone music from West Africa again and tell me if you hear lots of different rhythms or just a steady beat. Pat the beat on your lap to help you figure out the answer."
2. Play track.
3. Discuss answers (lots of different rhythms).
4. "Let's try to make some different rhythms in our class. Half of you will pat a steady beat on your lap, and half of you will do a two-finger tap to one of the xylophone rhythms (ti-ti ti-ti ta rest)."

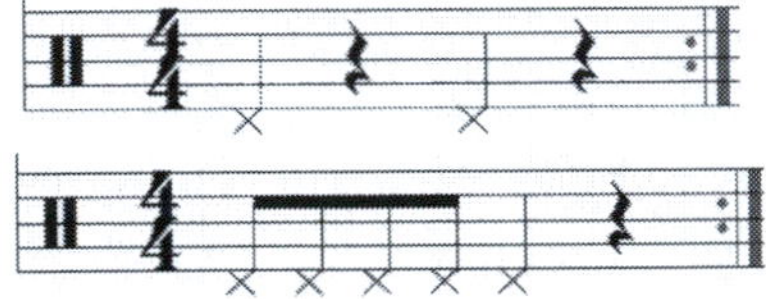

5. Divide class in half and assign task.
6. Play track.
7. Model steady beat for one group.
8. Model rhythm pattern for the other group.
9. Repeat, trading roles.

X Marks the Spot: Xylophones of West Africa

(For Enactive Listening)

Specific Use: Ages 5 to 7

Materials:

- "Tera Xylophone," Music from the Villages of Northeastern Nigeria, Smithsonian Folkways, Boomwhackers (Ab, Db, Eb), color-coded paper to match Boomwhackers, tone bells (Db, Eb, F, Ab, Bb), photograph of West African xylophone

Procedure:

1. "You all did a great job patting the steady beat and tapping the xylophone rhythm pattern. Instead of tapping our hands or patting our laps, let's add some instruments."
2. Divide children into steady beat group and rhythm pattern group.
3. Distribute Ab and Db Boomwhackers to steady beat group.
4. Play track.
5. Steady beat group plays their instruments.

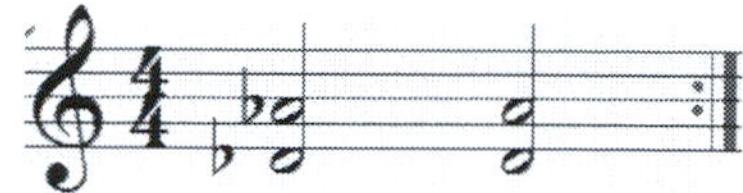

6. Distribute additional Db Boomwhackers and Eb Boomwhackers.
7. Use color-coded paper to rehearse the rhythm/tonal pattern.

8. Play track.
9. Steady beat group begins.
10. Rhythm pattern group is layered in.

X Marks the Spot: Xylophones of West Africa

(For Improvisation)

Specific Use: Ages 5 to 7

Materials:

- "Tera Xylophone," Music from the Villages of Northeastern Nigeria, Smithsonian Folkways, Boomwhackers (Ab, Db, Eb), tone bells (Db, Eb, F, Ab, Bb), photograph of West African xylophone

Procedures:

1. "Listen to my piece of music and raise your hand when you remember the name of this musical instrument and where in the world it comes from."
2. Play track.

3. Field student answers (xylophone, Nigeria, Africa).
4. "In some musical cultures in the world, people might make up what they are playing on the spot. That might sound funny, but it has a fancy name called 'improvisation.' That does not mean you make up things that are silly or that do not fit with the music. It means that you use the music as a guide to make up your own things that go with the music. You can have a chance to improvise, too, using the tone bells and Boomwhackers. Try to make your improvisation fit with the music—you can match how soft or loud, how fast or slow, or how choppy or smooth the music is."
5. Distribute instruments.
6. Play track. Children improvise.
7. Repeat as desired.

X Marks the Spot: Xylophones of West Africa

(For Integrating)

Specific Use: Ages 5 to 7

Materials:

- "Tera Xylophone," Music from the Villages of Northeastern Nigeria, Smithsonian Folkways, paper, pieces of colored tissue paper cut into small squares, glue

Procedure:

1. "We talked about how our xylophone music from West Africa has lots of different layers of sound. We can give that a fancy musical name called 'polyrhythm.' Let's create a piece of art that also has different layers, but instead of layers of sound it will be layers of colors."
2. Demonstrate how to glue pieces of tissue paper to the paper. Layer colors on top of other colors to create new shades and combinations.
3. Distribute paper, tissue paper squares, and glue to children.
4. Supervise and assist as they create their own layered collages.

Appendix 2

References and Resources

100 Basic Signs (Sign Language). Retrieved from www.lifeprint.com/asl101/pages-layout/concepts.htm

African Xylophones. Retrieved from https://vimeo.com/3515667

Alameida, R. K. (1997). *Nāmo'olelo Hawai'i o ka wā kahiko: Stories of old Hawai'i*. Honolulu, HI: The Bess Press.

Anderson, W. M. & Campbell, P. S. (Eds.). (2010). *Multicultural perspectives in music education: Volume one* (3rd Ed.). Lanham, MD: Rowman & Littlefield Education.

Awake, My Soul: The Story of the Sacred Harp. Retrieved from http://awakemysoul.com/

Beamer, N. (1987). *Nā mele hula: A collection of Hawaiian hula chants*. Lā'ie, HI: The Jonathan Napela Center.

Berríos-Miranda, M. (2013). Musical childhoods across three generations from Puerto Rico to the USA. In P.S. Campbell and T. Wiggins (Eds.), *The Oxford handbook of children's musical cultures* (301-324). New York, NY: Oxford University Press.

Boynton, S. & Kok, R. (2006). *Musical childhoods and the cultures of youth*. Middletown, CT: Wesleyan University Press.

Bradford, L. L. (1978). *Sing it yourself: 220 pentatonic American folk songs*. Sherman Oaks, CA: Alfred Publishing Co., Inc.

Brinckmeyer, L. M. (2015). *Wander the world with warm-ups: 40 fun warm-ups using songs from 20 countries*. Milwaukee, WI: Shawnee Press.

Burns, S. (2017). *Music education through a Montessori lens: Every child has musical potential*. Retrieved from https://nafme.org/music-education-montessori-lens-every-child-musical-potential/

Burton, S. L. & Taggart, C. C. (Eds.). (2011). *Learning from young children: Research in early childhood music*. Lanham, MD: Rowman & Littlefield Education.

Campbell, P. S. (2008). *Tunes and grooves for music education: Music for classroom use*. Upper Saddle River, NJ: Pearson.

Campbell, P. S., McCullouth-Brabson, E., & Tucker, J. C. (1994). *Roots and branches: A legacy of multicultural music for children*. Danbury, CT: World Music Press.

Campbell, P. S. & Scott-Kassner, C. (2014). *Music in childhood* (4th Ed.). Belmont, CA: Thomson.

Eckroth-Riley, J. (2014). *Everyday improvisation: Interactive lessons for the music classroom*. Van Nuys, CA: Alfred.

Feierabend, J. (2003). *Fingerplays and action songs*. Chicago, IL: GIA Publications, Inc.

Feierabend, J. (2004). *Songs and rhymes with beat motions*. Chicago, IL: GIA Publications, Inc.

Gault, B. M. (2016). *Listen up! Fostering musicianship through active listening*. New York, NY: Oxford University Press.

Gillet, D. K. (1999). *The queen's songbook*. Honolulu, HI: Hui Hānai.

Gold, L. (2005). *Music in Bali*. New York, NY: Oxford University Press.

Gopnik, A., Meltzhoff, A., & Kuhl, P. K. (1999). *The scientist in the crib: What early learning tells us about the mind*. New York, NY Perennial.

Gordon, E. E. (2013). *Music learning theory for newborn and young children*. Chicago, IL: GIA Publications.

East, H. (1989). *The singing sack: 28 song-stories from around the world*. London: A&C Black.

Erdei, P. (1974). *150 American folk songs to sing read and play*. London, UK: Boosey & Hawkes.

Hirsh-Pasek, K., Golinkoff, R. M., & Eyer, D. (2003). *Einstein never used flashcards*. Emmaus, PA: Rodale.

History of Steelpan. Retrieved from www.bbc.com/news/magazine-18903131

Ho'omāka'ika'i Staff. (2007). *Explorations! Ho'omāka'ika'i* (4th Ed.). Honolulu, HI: Kamehameha Schools Press.

Hula Performance by the Halau 'O Kekuhi Hula Ensemble. Retrieved from www.folkways.si.edu/hula-performance-halau-o-kekuhi-ensemble-big-island-hawaii/music/video/smithsonian

Ilari, B. (2013). Musical cultures of girls in the Brazilian Amazon. In P.S. Campbell and T. Wiggins (Eds.), *The Oxford handbook of children's musical cultures* (131-146). New York, NY: Oxford University Press.

The Invaders Steelpan Ensemble. Retrieved from www.invaders-tt.com/

Knapp, M. & Knapp, H. (1978). *One potato, two potato: The folklore of American children*. New York, NY: Norton.

KODO Taiko Performing Ensemble "Spirited Summer". Retrieved from www.kodo.or.jp/en/

Koops, L. H. (2013). Enjoyment and socialization in Gambian children's music making. In P.S. Campbell and T. Wiggins (Eds.), *The Oxford handbook of children's musical cultures* (266-281). New York, NY: Oxford University Press.

Kroll, V. & Lopez, L. (2006). *Uno, dos, tres, Posadas!* New York, NY: Puffin Books.

Ladysmith Black Mambazo. Retrieved from www.mambazo.com/

Langstaff, N. & Langstaff, J. (1986). *Sally go round the moon.* Watertown, MA: Revels, Inc. Publications.

Lind, V. R. & McKoy, C. (2016). *Culturally responsive teaching in music education: From understanding to application.* New York, NY: Routledge.

Li-Qiong, Y. & Cheng-Lang, Z. (2007). *A New Year's reunion.* Somerville, MA: Candlewick Press.

Loong, C. (2016). *Ni hao! Sing and chant your way to China!* Mentor, OH: Impel Training.

Marsh, K. (2008). *The musical playground: Global tradition and change in children's songs and games*. New York, NY: Oxford University Press.

Marsh, K. & Young, S. (2015). Musical play. In G. E. McPherson (Ed.), *The child as musician: A handbook of musical development* (2nd Ed.). New York, NY: Oxford University Press.

McPherson, G. E. (Ed.). (2015). *The child as musician: A handbook of musical development* (2nd Ed.). New York, NY: Oxford University Press.

Modern Maori Quartet, "Moli Hua". Retrieved from http://modernmaoriquartet.nz/video-archive/

"Oh, John the Rabbit" by Elizabeth Mitchell from *Sunny Day*. Retrieved from www.folkways.si.edu/oh-john-rabbit/american-folk-childrens/music/video/smithsonian

Opie, P. & Opie, I. (1969). *Children's games in street and playground.* New York, NY: Oxford University Press.

Pete Seeger: The power of song. Retrieved from www.pbs.org/video/american-masters-pete-seeger-power-song/

Schippers, H. (2010). *Facing the music: Shaping music education from a global perspective*. New York, NY: Oxford University Press.

Seeger, R. C. (1948). *American folk songs for children.* New York, NY: Oak Publications.

Shankar, R. *On appreciation of Indian classical music*. Retrieved from www.ravishankar.org/-music.html

Sheehy, D. (2005). *Mariachi music in America*. New York, NY: Oxford University Press.

Small, C. (1998). *Musicking*. Middletown, CT: Wesleyan University Press.

Smithsonian Folkways. Retrieved from www.folkways.si.edu/

Suzuki, S. (2015). *Nurtured by love: The classic approach to talent education* (2nd ed.). Miami, FL: Summy-Birchard, Inc.

Talbot, B. C. & Taro, M. (2017). *Gendeng rare: Children's songs and games from Bali*. Chicago, IL: GIA Publications, Inc.

Turino, T. (2008). *Music in the Andes*. New York, NY: Oxford University Press.

Valerio, W. H., Reynolds, A. M., Bolton, B. M., Taggart, C. C., & Gordon, E. E. (1998). *Music play*. Chicago, IL: GIA Publications, Inc.

Volk, T. M. (1998). *Music, education, and multiculturalism: Foundations and principles*. New York, NY: Oxford University Press.

Wade, B. C. (2004). *Thinking musically*. New York, NY: Oxford University Press.

Wade, B. C. (2005). *Music in Japan*. New York, NY: Oxford University Press.

What Makes a Good Mariachi? Retrieved from www.folkways.si.edu/what-makes-good-mariachi/latin-spoken-word-world/music/video/smithsonian

Index